Secret Symbolism
of the Tarot

Doris Chase Doane

Copyright 1993 by Doris Chase Doane

No part of this book may be reproduced or transcribed in any form or by any means, electronic or mechanical, including photocopying or recording or by any information storage and retrieval system without written permission from the author and publisher, except in the case of brief quotations embodied in critical reviews and articles. Requests and inquiries may be mailed to: American Federation of Astrologers, Inc., 6535 S. Rural Road, Tempe, AZ 85283.

ISBN-10: 0-86690-430-1
ISBN-13: 978-0-86690-430-8

Cover Design: Jack Cipolla

Published by:
American Federation of Astrologers, Inc.
6535 S. Rural Road
Tempe, AZ 85283

Printed in the United States of America

Dedication

I wish to express my grateful thanks to
the late Elbert Benjamine, who under the
pen name of C.C. Zain, wrote
The Sacred Tarot.
*He encouraged me to write books and
articles illustrating the
Religion of the Stars and
the Brother of Light teachings.*

Contents

I The Royal Path	1
II Law of Polarity	7
III Marriage of Cosmic Forces	13
IV Magnetism and Creative Energies	19
V The Five Pointed Star	25
VI Temptation of Two Paths	31
VII A Spiritual Pilgrimage	37
VIII Importance of Balance	45
IX Keys to Self Development	51
X Change and Destiny	57
XI The Touchstone of Purity	63
XII Above and Beyond Belief	71
XIII Aquarian Age Conditions	77
XIV Fluxing Polar Opposites	83
XV The Mark of the Beast	91
XVI Aggression in Spirituality	97
XVII Kinship of All Life	103
XVIII Controlling Occult Forces	109
XIX Love and Soul Development	115

XX Immortality of the Soul	121
XXI Spiritual Pathway to Adeptship	127
XXII The Neophyte's Illumination	133
XXIII Astrology and the Minor Arcana	139
XXIV Divinatory Significance	145
XXV The Tarot Face Cards	155

Foreword

Who am I? Where did I come from? Where am I going? These are a few of the questions which distinguish an aspirant on the path to self-knowledge from the unexamined life. Contained within these inquiries we see the compelling desire to understand the nature of the indiviudal and its relationship to the rest of creation. Religious and mystical systems have been developed from the time of our prehistoric ancestors to the present day in an effort to answer these very questions.

During the past decade we have witnessed an accelerated effort on behalf of enlightened men and women to break out of the confines of both academic and religious orthodoxy to investigate the so-called primitive religions of native cultures as well as the mystery schools of pre-Christian origins. At the roots of these varied traditions are the unique process of approaching one's relationship to deity through observing natural law and experiencing one's inter-connectedness to life.

In order to understand the individual's position in relationship to the universal whole, the ancient ones studied the heavens and their influence upon the seasons and other wordly events. The precise timing of stellar phenomena influenced the dates and characteristics of the world's major religious holidays and became the means by which we mark the passage of time with calendars and clocks. These astrological influences became veiled in the language of folklore, mythology, religion and the complex symbolism of mystery school initiation. Symbolism, both aesthetic and ceremonial, affects the subconscious of everyone to such a degree that the soul communicates to the conscious mind through the language of symbolism. The tarot archetypes were one of the means by which those spiritually evolved persons of the past sought to expound through the language of universal symbolism the mission of the soul and the influence of the stars.

Author Doris Chase Doane is no stranger to either astrology, tarot or religion. Her intellectual forays into each of these areas of study spans over 50 years. Her interest in comparative religions and philosophy began at an early age and eventually led to her fruitful relationship as a student and colleague of the spiritually distinguished author and teacher C.C. Zain (Elbert Bejamine). As author of more than 20 books and as president of the American Federation of Astrologers, Doris Chase Doane has become a major proponent of the study and acceptance of astrology throughout the United States and the world.

In *Secret Symbolism of the Tarot* the author takes the student on a spiritual journey through the tarot and explores the subject as a path toward the development of the Soul. She describes the tarot cards and reveals their relationship to initiation, Bible study and the esoteric meaning of numbers. She unveils the astrological significance of the tarot in a way that illumines the beginning student and provides insights for the advanced apprentice. By studying this enjoyable text the reader can uncover the means of gaining knowledge of future events and can encounter a philosophy dedicated to happy, constructive living.

Rev. Christopher Gibson
President, The Church of Light
Los Angeles, California, 1993

Chapter I

The Royal Path Of Life

It was not until 1919 that the facts of the Egyptian Tarot were given to the public. Up to that time, the information was kept secret. So secret, in fact, that so conscientious a mystical writer as A.E. Waite in the *Key to the Tarot* wrote: "We have now seen that there is no particle of evidence for the Egyptian origin of Tarot cards."

Public presentation appeared in the Brotherhood of Light Lessons in 1919 for the first time. C.C. Zain wrote in *The Sacred Tarot:* "From this (authorities and their works listed) it might be concluded that little is left to be said about the Tarot, but unfortunately for the general public the secret schools have had no intention of permitting real knowledge concerning it to escape from their mist. Consequently, much that has been written about the tarot has been, not for the purpose of making clear its significance, but to reveal what had clandestinely escaped from the secret schools. Even so fearless a writer as Elipha Levi admits this, and the few mistakes he makes in his own writings are so glaring, and yet so near the truth, that they can be ascribed neither to carelessness nor ignorance."

Tradition holds that information was handed down by word of mouth from the times of the Golden Age. These allegorical stories are an essential part of the wisdom which comes down to us from those ancient continents which sank: Atlantis and Mu. In fact, the Priests of Stellar Wisdom saw the approaching cataclysm by consulting astrological cycles and urged some of their learned members to establish colonies which later became the seven ancient centers of civilization: Egypt, India, Crete, Peru, Mexico, China and Chaldea.

In Egypt the ancient wise men specialized extensively in two things: astrology and the knowledge about the human soul. In so doing they developed extrasensory perception to a high degree, but they also kept laborious records day after day to verify their psychic findings.

These magi coupled their spiritual findings with astrology. Thus astrology to them was not only a means for character-reading, but it was viewed as the science to the soul, and the key to its possibilities. Their investigations revealed correspondences between spiritual ideas, numbers, and astrological symbols. To assist them in their work, these symbols representing a definite spiritual concept, were engraved on stone plates. These records were the result of impressions via ESP which were checked by exoteric observation and embraced a true spiritual science.

The Egyptians called the plates containing the language of universal symbolism the Royal Path of Life, because they set forth the spiritual heights to which a soul could reach. *TAR* means path, and

RO means royal in Egyptian. Through this association, the plates became known as the tarot.

There are a great many different tarot cards on the market today. As the physical and psychical aspects of life change in the stress and strain through history, so also does the symbolism on many of these packs of cards change. Outstanding examples are those of Pappus and those of the European Gypsies. Because of the association, however, these cards are best for those peoples.

They are closely associated with the Piscean Age beliefs and religion. It seems quite certain that activities of the secret brotherhood on the Inner Plane, by keeping the knowledge of the Egyptian Tarot from the public, were intentional. This action was taken so that this system which is as astrological as Uranus and embraces universal symbolism would be preserved untainted for presentation in the Aquarian Age.

This book is written to bring to a larger audience an understanding of the symbolism of the 22 Major Arcana of the Egyptian tarot. Permission has been granted to reproduce the replicas of the 22 pictures which were first carved on slate to repose on the walls of the Egyptian Temple of Initiation thousands of years ago.

There are 78 cards in a pack of Tarot cards. They include those corresponding to some astrological subdivision of the original 22 Major Arcana, which in turn are replicas of ideas tied in with the 10 planets and the 12 signs of the zodiac.

If you notice that the significance and attribution of numbers are different in the Egyptian tarot cards, do not be perturbed. For the reasons given above this is to be expected. The basic key-note of an astrological cycle or age accounts in part for the difference.

Major Arcanum I is called THE MAGUS. The three letters at the bottom of the illustration are (1-r) Aleph (Hebrew), a (English), and Athiem (Egyptian). At the top we find the corresponding number to be 1. The Roman numeral I designates the number of the Major Arcana, and the astrological correspondence of the card is the planet Mercury.

It is fitting for the Magus to represent the first Major Arcanum. Here we have the foundation. One is the number that represents the absolute, because all measurements start from it. All must also return to one which is the whole. Thus the idea of number 1 expresses the law of conservation of energy and the indestructibility of matter.

A Magus is one skilled in magic, which comes about mainly through the creation and vitalization of mental images. The card shows a perfect man, one who is in command of all his faculties. He is shown in a standing position to portray the fact that attitude of will always comes before any action is taken.

His robe is white to symbolize purity, virgin or acquired. Girdling the robe is a serpent biting his own tail, meaning man has eternity to attain his spiritual goal. As gold signifies light, a band of it encircles his forehead to show that all created things gravitate in the universal circumference.

In his right hand he holds a scepter of gold (light) with a circle atop it, representing spirit. The right hand is positive and he holds the scepter aloft with it in the sign of aspiration to science, wisdom and force. The star with its rays shooting up at the top of the card represents his spiritual master who directs and counsels him on his upward journey.

To show that man's mission is to subjugate the material world, his negative left-hand index finger points to the earth. The physical posture of the Magus (a man standing in command of his faculties, guided by spirit, with the right hand aloft and the left toward earth) shows that the human will should reflect the Divine Will in order to prevent evil and attract good.

In the lower right-hand corner of the card is a cubic stone, upon which rest a cup, a sword and a gold coin with a cross on it. The cup represents passions, both for unhappiness (slaves to emotion) or for happiness (masters of emotion). The sword signifies work and struggle in the face of the tests and trails given us. The coin portrays work accomplished and power gained through the exercise of will. The cross within the coin is the infinite seal and represents a spiritual transmutation of the power.

The cube itself represents the physical world. The ibis on the side of the cube symbolizes that eternal vigilance is needed if we are to surmount physical limitations.

Biblical significance of the Magus, Arcanum I, will be found in Revelation 22:13: I am the Alpha and Omega, the beginning and the end, the first and the last. In the Old Testament the same principal of creative activity and foundation is found in Genesis 1:1: In the beginning God created the heaven and the earth.

Mercury in astrology is always tied in with mind, question, thinking and the like. Therefore, Arcanum I indicates how important it is to make careful and thorough preparations for any demonstration. Before beginning, every law involved and all the tools to be used should be understood. In demonstration, or magic as it is also called, the potentialities of both planes are brought into play in an active and intense manner. Knowledge is protection.

As the card shows, the scepter in the positive right hand means intelligence on either plane, and the star above the Magus signifies the help of an inner-plane entity to assist in bringing about the end sought.

In relation to the initiation of the soul, Arcanum I represents the neophyte who has made an irrevocable decision to travel the pathway of the spirit. He has learned the illusion of matter and the transitory value of things material and decides to travel to adeptship.

Through the mercurial association, the shining fact shown to him is that he can travel that pathway only through his own efforts. No one else can do it for him. The guiding intelligence is there to help if he does use his will to take constructive action. His lofty aspirations for science, wisdom and power, as represented by the scepter being raised in the right hand, lift his vibrations, enabling him to tune in on the spiritual master, as represented by the star.

Chapter II

Law Of Polarity

Polarity consists of the qualities of exerting an attractive power in certain directions and of exerting a repellent power in other directions. If at the point of differentiation, all souls were stamped by Divine design with the same polarity, they would all tend to attract the same things to themselves because the experiences of life are attracted as they correspond to the polarity of the soul.

If we look about us at all types of life-forms including man, the one outstanding factor is that no two seem to have just the same experiences. The reason is fully explained by this Law of Polarity. The soul is endowed with attractive and repellent qualities when it is called into existence. Because of these qualities it attracts events that another soul does not attract, and it avoids types of events that another soul does attract. Therefore, the cosmic reason for being differs with each soul that has been brought into existence to fulfill a definite need in the Divine Plan. The second tarot card pictures the polarity principle.

Major Arcanum II is called VEILED ISIS. The three letters at the bottom of the illustration are (1-r) Beth (Hebrew), B (English), and Beinthin (Egyptian). At the top we find the corresponding number to be two. The Roman numeral II designates the number of the Major Arcanum, and the astrological correspondence of the card is the zodiacal sign of Virgo.

Polarity is expressed by number two, suggesting day and night, heat and cold, positive and negative. In all existence polarity is found to be evident. Even truth is dual. There is the truth of reality and the truth of appearance, esoteric and exoteric. While the number one expresses the law of the conservation of energy and the indestructibility of matter, the idea of number two expresses as the polarity of all matter.

VEILED ISIS represents the immaculate virgin, who through union with the holy spirit becomes a mother. In this aspect she is sitting at the portals of Nature's temple, veiling the wisdom which can be acquired only through union. This Arcanum represents science, embracing the harvest of experiences that have through assimilation become knowledge. A scientific sign of the zodiac, Virgo governs both the harvest and the process of assimilation before the harvest.

In the illustration a woman is seated at the threshold of the Temple of Isis. The two columns between which she is seated show duality as well as the polarity of the number two. One column appears darker than the other. The column on the woman's right is colored red to symbolize pure spirit and its higher than matter vibration. To the left is a black column, representing the bondage of matter over the gross and impure nature.

Did you notice the lady's beautiful tiara? It has three stories and is topped by the lunar crescent. The veil which covers her face is attached to her crowning tiara. The mantle that is draped from her shoulder half covers the open book that rests upon her knees. Symbolically, the half-draped volume signifies occult science, a subject all initiates encounter at the threshold of the sanctuary of Isis. When the neophyte studies occult science, he is told the secrets of universal nature.

Symbol of Mercury (Hermes) upon the bosom of the Virgin signifies that matter is fertilized by spirit to insure the evolution of mind, or soul. The two bottom factors of Mercury, the cross and the circle, are surmounted by the third factor: The lunar crescent. The cross represents matter and the circle symbolizes spirit. Together they figure the lingam of the Hindus, representing the union of the sexes.

The crescent topping the cross and the circle represents the soul which is the evolved product of the union of spirit and matter. The seal on the breast of Nature also indicates that knowledge comes from God and is limitless.

Key to the Arcanum is the veil falling over the face of Isis. It signifies that Nature gives her gems of truth to the pure in heart only. She hides her truths from the sensation seeker and the vulgar. Again we see duality.

Polarity is expressed by the book being half hidden under the mantle. Half the truth can be learned by the physical senses, representing the exoteric aspect. The other half must be gotten through the psychic senses, the esoteric side. In fact, reason without intuition is limited to effects only. But when the reason is combined with intuition, a blend of the exoteric and esoteric, the neophyte is able to pull aside the mantle from Nature' innermost pages and probe her mysteries at length.

You may ask, just what are the psychic senses? They are the astral counterparts, the inner-plane expression, of the physical senses. The ancient Magi included thought transference and intuition with the physical senses, making a total of seven physical senses. Here are the psychic correspondences:

Physical Sense	Psychic Sense
Touch	Psychometry
Taste	Absorption of Ethereal Energies
Smell	Sensing the Spiritual Aromas
Sight	Clairvoyance
Hearing	Clairaudience
Intuition	Inspiration
Thought Transference	Spirit Communion

If a neophyte wishes to attain complete spiritual adjustment, it is necessary that he use both the physical senses and the psychic senses. This is so because complete knowledge is the product from the union of information from both the inner plane and the outer plane.

Pages of Nature's book reveal the secret mysteries only to the student who meditates in silence. Not a passive meditation, but one where he remains in full and calm possession of himself. Note the three stories on the tiara which crowns Isis. They have an important significance. The ensemble indicates that the power of the intellect can probe the three realms of existence; physical, astral and spiritual.

Indicating the feminine attribute is the lunar crescent, topping the tiara. In occult science intelligence should be guided by the intuitive or psychic powers. The rational mind is masculine and should be guided by the feminine (psychic) qualities, thus completing the polarity.

As the card portrays, the woman is seated, not standing or leaning, to signify that will (Arcanum I) united to science is immovable.

Biblical significance of Veiled Isis, Arcanum II, can be seen in the story of the Virgin Mary. The immaculate conception was familiar to very ancient nations long before Christianity. In Egypt it was taught that Isis, conceiving immaculately, gave birth to Horus, the Sun God. The Egyptian Virgin is often pictured with the New Moon in her arms. At one time the Jews were held captive in Egypt. While there they learned of the traditional lore. When Isis became an object of Christian adoration, they substituted the baby Jesus for the New Moon.

Immaculate conception has an esoteric meaning. Matter (the feminine principle in nature) is impregnated by spirit (the positive principle), and the resultant gestation is evolution. This gives birth to man, who has an immortal soul as well as the potentiality of attaining adeptship.

Symbolism in Arcanum I revealed to us the importance of making thorough preparation before any feat of magic is attempted. While Arcanum II symbolizes the principle of reception, it is the polar opposite of the former principle of Arcanum I. Reception is the feminine reaction of the magical agent, and it teaches us the androgyne nature of the astral light.

One of the best examples of this principle is the psychic phenomena brought about by mental means. Organic electromagnetism tends to take whatever form or action it is directed to by the intelligences associated with it. The movement of physical objects by mental energy (such as the dice experiments carried out at Duke University to illustrate the psychokinetic effect) depends upon a sufficient volume of organic electromagnetism to make successful contact and direction.

Electromagnetism is the magical medium which acts as the connecting link between mind and matter. In order to affect material conditions by the mind, it must be present in sufficient volume. This is explained in detail in *Laws of Occultism*.

Polarity of Arcanum II is also pointed up in the initiation, where the pilgrimage of the soul reaches a definite level both in the descending and ascending arc of the evolutionary cycle.

The evolutionary cycle represents the differentiation of the twin souls of the one ego into opposite polarities. This activity takes place in the highest spiritual realm, just before the fall of the twin souls into the realm of material conditions.

Arcanum II represents that point in initiation where the soul realizes that man or woman alone is not complete. A soul of the opposite sex is needed. At this point in evolution, the soul also comes to the illuminating realization that reason alone is not enough to reach adeptship. Intuition and the development of the psychic senses are necessary and completes the Law of Polarity.

Chapter III

MARRIAGE OF COSMIC FORCES

Progressing beyond the polarity principle, we shall see that all positive and negative forces come into union and manifest at the third angle of the triangle of existence.

Electricity and magnetism are the result of positive and negative forces trying to unite. In fact, analysis of every force in the universe would reveal some similar attraction. There is a marriage of cosmic forces.

A good example is chemical affinity. It results in the marriage of atoms. Some atoms get the urge to divorce partners with whom they do not get along so well. Then they marry other atoms who have a greater attraction for them. When you pause and think you will see that we use the power generated from these marriages for many things, to drive locomotives or to take us about in our cars.

Breathing is also dual. Inhalations and exhalations. Positive and negative. In the process there is another marriage of cosmic forces. In addition to oxygen being applied to the blood, electromagnetic energies are absorbed and carried to the nerves, brain, and electromagnetic body. This third Major Arcanum card represents union.

Major Arcanum III is called ISIS UNVEILED. In the illustration the three letters at the bottom are (1-r) Gimel (Hebrew), G (English), and Gomer (Egyptian). At the top we find the corresponding number to be three. The Roman numeral III designates the number of the Major Arcanum, the astrological correspondence of the card is the zodiacal sign Libra.

Natural ruler of all partnerships, the zodiacal sign of Libra pictures astrologically the union of summer and winter. It is also the union in the story of the fall of Eve, when she was tempted by the serpent of desire to get experience, to want children.

But Arcanum III pictures more than the union of two forces. It also embraces the enlightenment which follows after union. Adam and Eve found their range of mental activity was increased markedly due to their union.

Number three is expressed as the union of polar opposites. It is the relation between such forces that cause vibration and change. Thus, three is the union of different polarities back of all life, all action and all intelligence.

Standing out in the illustration of Arcanum III is the huge radiant Sun. It is not a coincidence that 30 rays emanate from its glowing orb. These 30 rays correspond to the number of degrees in one sign of the zodiac.

Sitting within the Sun, a woman wears a crown of twelve stars. Thus is represented the passage of the Sun through the 12 signs of the zodiac each year. This picture in its essence also represents the union of cosmic forces.

The feminine principle is depicted by the Moon upon which Isis rests her feet. The cube where she sits is the cross of matter. Here the rays of the Sun and Moon meet, signifying the union of male and female forces.

Again, we find a serpent in the illustration. This time it is a sacred serpent that circles Isis' brow, with its head flung upward. It is a symbol of enlightenment.

In her right hand she holds a scepter with globe at the top of it. As a phallas, it is the indication of the ever-borning principle: The eternal action of creative energy upon everything already born or yet to be born. An eagle rests in her left hand. It is a symbol of fruitfulness well as representing the heights (eagles fly extremely high) to which the spirit can raise itself through the emotions at the time of union.

Covered with eyes, the cube upon which Isis Unveiled is seated signifies that union opens the eyes of the soul to a knowledge of good and evil.

This whole picture represents generation, gestation, and universal fecundity. It is a symbolic presentation which can be easily understood by any peoples, regardless of what language they speak.

Biblical references of this Isis Unveiled is not only found in the fall of Eve and the resultant exclusion of the human race from the Garden of Eden, but it can also be found in the story of Noah's Ark. Its three stories correspond to the three realms of the Arcanum. They are represented by the Sun (spirit), the Moon (astral), and the cube (physical). The cube or physical world, the square cabin of the ark, is where the soul undergoes its period of gestation.

Many times through the Bible can be found the trinity of three. Nor is this trinity associated solely with Christianity. Its symbolism can be found in all other religions including the Religion of the Stars. The Babylonian trinity is Anu-Enlil-Ea (sky-earth-Water) and Sun-Shamash-Ishtar (Moon-Sun-star). The Brachmanic trinity is brahma (creator), Vishnu(preserver) and Siva (destroyer). Buddist is Sangha (monastic order), the Buddha (creator), and the Dharma (sacred law). The threefold principle is found in all sacred books, such as the Bible, Koran and the Upanishads.

In the art of demonstration, or magic, Arcanum III refers to the principle of vitalization. It is the intense vibratory affect of the interaction of polar opposites. For every positive force in the universe, there is an equal and negative force. It is impossible to make a magnet possessing just one pole due to this fundamental law.

Because a soul is a definite force in the cosmos and because a soul has a definite polarity, it is just as impossible to think of a soul of one polarity starting out on the tide of evolution without a similar soul of the other polarity as it is to think of a magnet with just one pole.

Except for its sex, or polarity, the female soul must be the exact replica of the male soul, because action and reaction are exactly the same. The only difference is the type of experiences each soul is called upon to meet. These experiences are not parallel. But the ultimate spirituality each soul gains from reacting to these experiences make one soul complement the other. The union of the twin souls constitutes a soul mate system.

In the occult sciences spiritual alchemy corresponds to Major Arcanum III. The spiritual alchemist uses each and every event in his life to create spiritual values. The reverberatory furnace he uses is composed of feeling that arises from unusual spiritual perception which embraces all life. This feeling gives rise to the knowledge that the universe is an organic whole and that the soul is one unit in the cosmic plan.

An intense desire to assist the progress of the whole, accompanied with a deep yearning to use every tool, faculty, or power to advance the welfare of all, gives the spiritual alchemist a spiritual understanding of the relation of his soul to the cosmic forces of the universe. Such a state of consciousness overflows the heart with sincere devotion to cosmic prosperity.

Only unselfish love can affect spiritual substance, where the spiritual body of man resides. Thus the reverberatory furnace of the spiritual alchemist is fed by an outpouring of love which meets and unites with other cosmic forces. The grain of pure gold within the soul is the ego. All souls are the seed of pure gold. Life depends upon love, and immortality comes from an enduring spiritual love. Just as the atoms of physical matter join in a chemical marriage, the spiritual thoughts, and aspirations join in a cosmic marriage to assist the soul in accomplishing the great work.

Arcanum III illustrates this parallel. The Sun exerts its greatest power when its rays are radiated vertically. In the picture, the Sun is above and denotes the masculine principle in nature. The Moon is seen most of the time at night, the opposite of the Sunny day. In the illustration the Moon is at the opposite position of the Sun, at the feet of Isis Unveiled. This position indicates a passive, inert principle. Its horizontal placement emphasizes the symbolism of the eternal feminine.

The cube is likened to the cross of matter, or to the earth which is considered as the womb of nature. Isis Unveiled sits at this point of union. Here the masculine, electric rays of the Sun are embraced by the feminine, magnetic rays of the Moon. This solar-lunar union is but another marriage of cosmic forces.

Chapter IV

Magnetism and Creative Energies

What a splendid and inspiring sight the Egyptian Temple of Initiation must have been thousands of years ago! The wise men had placed on the walls stone tablets depicting the 22 Major Arcana of the tarot. Each tablet not only told the story in universal symbolism of the stellar religion. It went further to give a well-rounded philosophy which was easy to apply in the neophyte's daily life. To these sages life embraced two planes of existence: The inner and the outer.

Arcanum IV gave information on the occult science called Imponderable Forces. It is the science which considers all the invisible energies not recognized by material science. But its particular domain is in the principles of ceremonial magic, where ritual and prepared equipment are used to get certain results, as well as the proper use and direction of creative energies. A study of the symbolism on this tarot card will lead to fuller understanding of what the ancients wanted to tell.

In the Egyptian tarot Major Arcanum IV is called THE SOVEREIGN. The three letters you see at the bottom of the illustration are (1-r) Daleth (Hebrew), D (English), and Denian (Egyptian). At the top we will find the corresponding number to be four, the Roman numeral IV designates the number of the Major Arcanum. The astrological correspondence of the card is the zodiacal sign of Scorpio.

The result of action is expressed by the number four. it is the fruit of the work indicated by three. In other words, realization comes from effort. Here is typified life springing into manifestation as the result of the union of polar opposites. In this sense four represents the practical, because it is concrete and has form.

Symbolically it tells the neophyte that the universal truth depends upon viewpoint. It shows that each realm is actual when viewed from its own plane.

By this symbolism the wise ones told the lesson and pictured the practical approach by applying this symbology to everyday living and affairs.

As above; so below! Every tarot card follows this corresponding pattern. In the macrocosm (universe) four signifies the knowledge that comes through experience. Scientifically, four relates to all laws which govern the effective use of energy, and to the laws that govern the things produced as a result of the motion.

There are many passages in the Bible that refer to Arcanum IV, because four is the number of fruitfulness. Throughout Biblical stories fruitfulness is looked upon as a virtue, while barrenness is considered a crime. The ancients taught that the principles of fruitfulness applied more importantly to the mental plane. Immediately we can see why they thought as they did. When man is barren of thought, his progress ceases, and his physical body starts to decay.

Fruitfulness of the sign Scorpio is detected in the following two verses from the Bible:

Gen. 1:28: "And God blessed them, and God said unto them. Be fruitful and multiply, and replenish the earth, and subdue it; and have dominion over the fish of the sea, and the fowl of the air, and over every living thing that moveth upon the earth."

Rev. 12:5: "And she brought forth a man child, who was to rule all nations with a rod of iron; and her child was caught up unto God and his Throne." This passage is ripe with Scorpio symbolism as the picture on Arcanum IV shows.

A man wearing a sovereign helmet is seen. He sits on a cubic stone, with his right hand raising a scepter which is topped by a circle. His right leg is bent, making a cross as it rests upon his other leg.

In this portrayal the cubic stone, image of the perfect solid, indicates labor which has reached completion. Notice the cat on the side of the stone. The ancient magi placed it there to tell the neophyte that the vision of the soul penetrates the illusions of matter.

The helmet on his head emblemizes force conquered by power. He holds the scepter of Isis, showing that he has knowledge of the spiritual use of creative energies. He points his left hand down, to mean that he uses these energies in subjugating the physical; ". . . dominion over the fish of the sea, the fowl of the air . . . ."

Symbolizing enlightenment is the sacred serpent at his brow. A hawk appears on the front of his garment. This bird is sacred to the Sun, and in the illustration it typifies his soaring ambition to build up a tremendous spiritual growth.

His apron plus his crossed legs form a trine above a cross. The cross is the emblem of the four elemental kingdoms he has mastered, resulting in the expansion of human power his new understanding allows him. The trine above symbolizes mind dominating matter and the conservation of energy, a principle seen in all chapters of Mother Nature's book.

Topping the scepter is the circle which represents the soul that has evolved as a result of his applied experience and knowledge to the physical plane at which he points his left hand.

After analyzing the various symbolical patterns of Arcanum IV, the true significance of the passage from Revelations, quoted above, is apparent. Reread it and see the fruitfulness of Scorpio. Mars, its ruler, governs iron. The rod in the sovereign's hand shows the dominating character as well as the possibilities of spiritual realization, symbolized by the hawk, for the child was caught up to the throne of God. The hawk flies toward the Sun.

Sex is back of all energy. From a magnetic standpoint, Scorpio is the most potent sign of the zodiac. Thus Scorpio, due to its rulership of sex, more than any other sign is capable of receiving and transmitting the magnetic energies generated by man. These energies liberated through the fluxing of the polar opposites, when they are properly controlled as depicted by the illustration, are most important in the work of proper transmutation. Control is not found through repression but directing the energies into proper channels. Proper direction prevents an explosion which can cause considerable damage to man's two-plane organism.

Undirected forces, or the inversive and degenerative use of the principle is represented by the expression of the lower side of Pluto, co-ruler of the sign Scorpio.

There are many avenues through which we can develop spirituality. Perhaps the most potent of them all is through the affections. One of the most destructive forces comes from a union prompted by lust or selfishness. This is so because it is through the emotions that we are able to raise or lower our basic vibratory rates. In so doing we elevate ourselves to a high condition, or we degrade ourselves by slipping to a downward level, depending upon our attitude.

Intense emotional states which are usually associated with union arouse the creative energies. If they desire tenderness, kindness and the wish to help others, then these states work vigorously in aiding the mind to build spirituality. On the other hand, if they give rise to brutal thoughts and encourage grossness and coarseness by cultivating a lower vibratory rate, they tend to destroy spirituality.

In spite of the extreme tendency for its manifestation, there is no power that can lift the soul to such exalted states of ecstasy as love. Therefore, it is only through love that we can contact the higher spiritual states. God is love.

Suppression of affection helps no one. The emotions must be expressed. When a suitable channel is found for its expression, the emotion coupled with desire calls into play, through the Law of Association, factors which make possible the constructive use of the creative energies.

The sovereign of the tarot well depicts these influences. It expresses in the intellectual world of the realization of the ideas of sexual morality by the four-fold labors of the mind: affirmation, negation, discussion, and solution.

In the physical world, the Sovereign expresses as the realization of acts directed by the knowledge of truth, the love of justice, the force of will, and the works of the organs. Thus the ancient shows on the fourth tablet the lesson which corresponds to the zodiacal sign of Scorpio, ruler of magnetism and creative energies.

Chapter V

The Five-Pointed Star

Whether he knows it or not each person attracts to himself assistance on both planes, the outer and the inner. Beings which come to his aid are of the same character as the person. In other words, if the motive is high and follows the theme of contributing to life, the helpers, both visible and invisible, will have a high vibratory potential. But if the motive springs from selfishness and revenge, the opposite type will rush to the aid.

Many philosophers have stated that thought in one way or another: as a man thinketh so is he. The esoteric significance of the pentagram brings to light revealing points of interest to the simple phrase.

In other words, a person's dominant vibratory rate at any given time determines what he will attract. In the tarot, one becomes interested in reading the cards, but to assist in building spirituality and thus attract more happiness into the life, meditation on each Major Arcana will prove helpful for the neophyte. The esoteric, magical, or alchemical aspect of the cards places a key of enlightenment in the hand of those who will but use it. The illustration of the five-pointed star is one such key. In the Egyptian tarot, Major Arcanum V is called THE HIEROPHANT. at the bottom of the illustration you will note three letters (1-r) He (Hebrew), E (English) and Eni (Egyptian). at the top we find the corresponding number to be five. The Roman numeral V designates the number of the Major Arcana. The astrological correspondence of the card is Jupiter.

All of the apparent contradictions of nature are explained in the number five, because it unites the first four digits into a harmonious oneness, or unity. In other words, the Yod-He-Vau-He is composed of the One Principle, the One Law, the One Agent, and the One Truth, which are not independent factors but act in mutual benefit for one another.

These four ideas are also represented by the four animals standing at the gates of the heavens. Each quadrant of the sky represents one

of these ideas. They are depicted by the fixed sign of each quarter: Taurus, Leo, Scorpio, and Aquarius. These ideas are brought together into a fourfold form of a sphinx. In thus expressing the four parts of the zodiac, the constitution of man is symbolized. Five represents man or woman alone. There are five positive points from which electromagnetic fluid emanates. Two hands, two feet and the head are the five points of projection. Health depends in great part upon the equal distribution to these five points of the vital energies. Because the soul of man has passed through the four lower (elemental) realms of his cycle of necessity and has thus reached a higher attainment, he becomes the rightful sovereign.

In viewing five from this angle, four plus one equals five indicating realization that has developed as a result of applying intelligence and will. It is because the neophyte has attained true manhood (or womanhood) - having had a wider experience from which to develop his personal potentials - that he directs the various entities, both physical and astral that function within the orbit of his existence. They become man's willing and obedient servants in proportion to the amount of spiritual supremacy the man has attained. The more spiritual he becomes, the more assistance he will gain from corresponding entities.

Students of Bible astrology find much of interest in the study of Arcanum V. Perhaps the outstanding part of the illustration is the pentagram, or five-pointed star, that the Hierophant makes with his right hand. As stated above, this is the symbol of man, of intellectual power that dominates the four elemental kingdoms. It is the symbol of the magical forces of the human will as well. Because the user is obedient to the Diefic Law, he gains force and thus identifies himself with the Divine power that permeates all things.

Many generations ago it was a five-pointed star shining in the heavens that beckoned the Three Wise Men. This blazing light was a conjunction of three planets according to modern day astronomers. It lead them to the new Sun-god so that they might worship him. Significantly, their gifts of gold, frankincense and myrrh represents the tree levels, or worlds, to which man has access; physical, astral, and spiritual. This triad is symbolized in the illustration by the triple tau in the left hand of the Hierophant.

The Bible tells a story which when viewed esoterically goes about so: The star of religious devotion lead the wise men into a knowledge of the three worlds and the laws of governing them. Then the wise men returned to their own country by another route. Wavering footsteps no longer existed. Because they had gained illumination, their pathway was direct and certain. It was the return of the spirit. They traveled the route of self-conscience immortality.

The Star of the East has the same significance as Arcanum V. It symbolizes Divine Law and Religion. I always think of this association when I see a star in print today. It appears frequently in newspapers and magazines, sometimes heading a column or being used to divide items in long columns. In its spiritual aspect, working from constructive motives, the star appears with the single point up. But when it is inverted, like a five-pointed star upside down, then we have a symbol embracing the opposite of Divine Law. It also carries the meaning of man governed by the opposite of intelligence.

The inverted five-pointed star represents chaos, evil inspiration, the devil, and the working of destructive forces. This is a good thing to know. As human beings are inspired by exactly the type of inner-plane intelligences that vibrate to their level of thinking. In this light, do you not think that the position of the star is revealing as to the motives of the hand that presents it?

Inversion of the star is likened to the Lamb of God that is transformed into the Goat of Mendes. In black magic, its expression is made by closing the hand so that two fingers are up, the horns of the goat or the feet of the man, instead of three, which represents the head and the two hands reaching for divine inspiration.

To fully understand the degree of mastership that all neophytes are working to attain, the use of divine force to quell elemental forces is represented by the pentagram and is pictured in Arcanum V.

A Hierophant, master of the sacred mysteries and occult science, is pictured on the card. He is seated between two columns of the sanctuary. He leans upon a cross of three bars, while making the sign of the pentagram. At his brow the sacred serpent thrusts its head. At his feet two men kneel. The illustration is in black and white, however one man is dressed in red and the other in black.

The genius of good inspiration, of mind and of conscience is representative of the free will to obey or to disobey the law.

In his left hand the triple tau, or crosses, symbolize divine fire that permeates the three worlds, spiritual, astral, and physical, so that everything in the universal life may have its birth (awakening). As the left hand is used, the negative hand, rapport and receptivity of the Divine source is indicated.

The right hand, or positive hand, makes the sign of the pentagram. In this action, he symbolizes the principles that Divine energy can be used to command the obedience of sub-mundane atoms of life, or to get assistance from the inner planes in helping to calm the passions and instincts of the flesh.

Here again as in earlier cards, the sacred serpent at the brow symbolizes enlightenment. The two kneeling men represent the forces of light and the forces of darkness, both of whom obey the pentagram.

After reading the foregoing, it should not be too difficult to understand why it is important to use the proper symbols in all invocations and in ceremonial magic. Rituals and symbols should be carefully studied before they are put into use to insure that they are designed to assist the progressive evolution of creation.

A most powerful magical token, the pentagram is the symbol of white magic. It represents the power of the mind that gives all of its energies to building for better conditions and thus employing the Divine Law in constructive endeavors.

As the symbols and rituals in magic or religion are closely associated with entities on the inner plane, you can see how important it is to know with just what you are dealing. Ignorance does not excuse anyone. If you put forces corresponding to astral gangsters into play, the law works to bring about just such contacts in spite of the fact that ignorance may have prompted the action in the first place. It is similar to tuning in your radio. When you turn the dial to KNX, you get KNX and not some other station.

In the initiation of the soul Arcanum V, symbolized by Jupiter, shows the point on the ascending life wave where the voice of conscience calls to the neophyte to turn his back on the flesh-pots and devote his efforts to things of the spirit which will add to the cosmic scheme of things. If he hears and heeds the call, he no longer lives for self alone. He views his every action in the cosmic light in his interesting search for his true relation to God and the universe.

Soon his consciousness is flooded for 24 hours a day with the idea of his own cosmic usefulness. He vibrates with the Grand Master and thus is able to be impressed by his inner-plane helpers to take the constructive path, and to use his inherited divine forces to further the Great Plan.

When the soul has assimilated the lessons of expansion depicted by Arcanum V, good fortune comes in the form of spiritual attainment which was not available before this step is taken. Masonry is the branch of occult science corresponding to this card. In its ancient aspect, masonry embraces the proper use of creative energies by sex as well as the evolution of the human soul as it manifests on the three planes of being: Physical, astral, and spiritual.

Jupiter is the planet of good fortune. Thus if the import of Arcanum V is embraced and used as a key, faith comes, uniting the human soul with its Maker, lifting his will and works to a higher plane. At the same time this will release his creative energies through constructive channels. This is the promise of the five-pointed star of the tarot.

Chapter VI

Temptation Of Two Paths

Every minute of our lives we are adding or subtracting energies which go to make our lives a success. Every emotional state, every thought, and every physical action lend their energies to this important determination. When we analyze our thoughts, feelings, and actions, it is hard to find a neutral ground.

At all times, to a greater or lesser degree, our energies are pouring through either constructive or destructive channels of expression. It is only when the sum total of the constructive energies build up a volume which far surpasses the destructive energies that we attain satisfactory accomplishment.

The temptation as pictured in the sixth tarot card is of daily (and indeed hourly) concern to anyone who expects to make the most of his life through the application of spiritual knowledge. Just as change is the only permanent fact in the universe, so is making decisions a permanent fact in our daily lives. A study of the tarot reveals the story of triumphing over temptation, which brings rewards of soul growth and great ability to contribute to the cosmic scheme of things.

Major Arcanum VI is called THE TWO PATHS. The three letters at the bottom of the illustration are (1-r) Vau (Hebrew), V-U-W (English) and Ur (Egyptian). At the top we find the corresponding number to be six. The Roman numeral VI designates the number of the Major Arcanum of the tarot. The astrological correspondence of this card in the planet Venus.

Number six signifies two actions (twice three). Rather than representing forces in balance, it indicates the vacillation between action and reaction. In this respect it denotes forces, either wavering or oscillating, or uncontrolled and wrongly directed that they have a tendency to destroy each other. Here the antidote of applying mental alchemy is the step toward correction. When Venus energies, represented by the number six, are expressing discordantly, the application of Saturn type thoughts on a high level will harness the undirected streams and point them in the direction of constructive endeavor through system and organization.

The Two Paths of Arcanum VI represent the test of power. Those who attain power, especially those who get their power through the use of invisible energies, always attract the brothers of the shadow.

As everything in the universe has a constructive purpose, these dark forces are the instruments of the Supreme Intelligence to place an opportunity before the progressing soul for overcoming temptation. In the overcoming, the soul is initiated into a high place of usefulness in the Divine Plan, due to having gained greater ability in the act of overcoming.

However, should those in power yield to the dictates of the dark ones, they soon become slaves of the very forces they thought they had under control. In another aspect this card represents the kinds of opportunities which develop the strength and will through obstacles, privation, and hardship.

In the illustration a man is standing at the point where two roads meet. With arms crossed upon his chest, he looks at the ground. He is faced with making a choice. Thus he pauses in contemplation.

Temptation is symbolized by two women, each one touches the man's shoulder and beckons him to follow her road. Modestly clothed, the woman on his right (positive side) personifies virtue. At her brow is seen the sacred serpent, which always signifies enlightenment. Wearing less clothing, the woman at his left (negative side) represents vice. She plays the role of temptress. Upon her head is a crown of leaves and the vine of the grape.

In this tableau, the ancients symbolized a struggle between conscience and passions. Whatever the road taken, in answer to the promptings of the animal soul or the call of the Divine soul, the result of the decisions starts a new period in life, a new path.

In the upper left hand corner of the illustration we see the genie of Justice surrounded by a flashing auriole of twelve rays. These indicate the 12 motivating principles as symbolized by the 12 signs of the zodiac. The genie placed within the auriole symbolizes that justice will be meted out in good time to every soul as the Sun passes through the zodiacal signs.

Directing his arrow of punishment toward the woman representing vice, he draws his bow and stands ready to take action if wrong decisions are made. Crowning the genie is the pointed flame of fire which represents spirit, counteraction for the temptress.

A knowledge of astrology is necessary to get the deepest and broadest understanding of the sacred tarot as presented by the ancient masons. It goes without saying that the best tarot card readers are those well versed in astrological factors. Arcanum VI is very important when considered from this angle. Its astrological correspondence is Venus. Did you ever stop to realize that Venus not only rules two signs of the zodiac, but also rules three zodiacal decanates in the earth signs and three decanates in the air signs. Thus six decanate sub-rulerships are allotted to Venus.

A decanate is a third of a sign or ten (decan) degrees. Each sign has three decantes: three times ten equals 30. There are two different ways to allot these decantes to the signs. Most popular is by allotting them according to the triplicities. Take Taurus: Venus for the first, Mercury for the second, and Saturn for the third. Thus going through the trinity of earth signs.

As we face the two pathways every day of our lives, we can take a lesson from the Venus tarot plate. After we have studied astrology for a time, we come to the knowledge that the circumstances of our lives are attracted to us because of the activity of the thought cells in our finer forms. Because the astral body is so responsible to every thought and emotion we have, it is often called the desire body. The kind of affections we have shape this finer form and nourish it. This takes place because it is composed of states of consciousness. Due to its receptive and yielding organization, our emotions play an important part in the building of it. This astral body corresponds to Venus.

Circumstances which we attract are just what we need for our own education in the cosmic plan. Often it seems as if we are imposed upon by nature or others without adequate cause. But we find when we face ourselves, the real I, the cause lies within us and stems from the decisions made while standing at the two pathways.

Our negative expression would be to complain of the injustices of life. But the positive and spiritual expression is to spend our energy to alter ourselves so that we can attract better fortune and escape the arrows of punishment meted out by the genie of justice.

Venus rules the affections and social relations. When Venus is stimulated by aspects in a horoscope, the thoughts turn to a love of ease, comfort, luxury and pleasure. These thoughts and feelings are not essentially evil. In fact, they should be built into the life in a constructive manner. But in seeking the line of least resistance they may lead into vice as symbolized by the temptress.

Should we fail to resist the importunities of the temptress, our decision leads to the negativeness that comes under Arcanum II, Vieled Isis. The resultant harvest we reap is described by Arcanum XV The Black Magician, which is the second decade of VI (six plus nine equals 15).

In the Bible this Arcanum is typified by Isaac and his two sons. Esau is the voice of vice that would cause man to sell his birth right (spiritual heritage) for a mess of potage (material things). Jacob is the voice of Virtue, the conscience that successfully wrestled with the spirit of temptation. Even though the struggle brought affliction, he was not conquered.

The passage giving a fine interpretation of this concept will be found in Matthew 4:8: "Again the devil taketh him up into the exceedingly high mountains, and shewth him all the kingdoms of the world and the glory of them; and said unto him, all these things will I give thee if thou wilt fall down and worship me."

Regardless of what problem we face to solve, what difficulty we need to overcome, or what decision we are called upon to make, Arcanum VI gives a clue to right action. We have parroted the phrase "God is love."

But do we really understand the esoteric significance behind that phrase? Venus represents these forces. Life depends upon love, and immortal life in a spiritual realm depends on an enduring spiritual love. It is this kind of universal love that all souls are striving to find, whether they know it or not. All souls are straining toward the expression of it. Through our daily decisions we are building tomorrow, as well as today. To insure happiness and spirituality love is needed. (See Spiritual Alchemy.[2])

Let us place our hand in that of the woman of virtue and tread with her the roadway of life, light and love by heeding the admonition of Arcanum VI in the Royal Path of Life.

Chapter VII

A Spiritual Pilgrimage

Sagittarius has natural rule over the ninth house in the horoscope. This department of life governs, among other things, long trips, religion, public expression and courts. Therefore, coming into the concept associated with this ninth sign of the zodiac are such words as fair play, honesty, judgment, righteousness, verity, audacity, and law. All these things are important to consider if one is to travel the spiritual pathway for any distance.

As was pointed out in the last chapter, every sign of the zodiac is divided into three decanates of 10 degrees each. In the case of Sagittarius, the first decanate is the Jupiter-Sagittarius decanate. C.C. Zain allotted appropriate keywords to these decanates. Here the keyword is *devotion*. It is only through devotional practice that we can tap the highest sources for assistance in this business of everyday living. The second decanate is sub-ruled by Mars-Aries, keyed by the word *exploration*. Here is the courageous fight to stand up against any and all odds for the just and the true.

Sun-Leo sub-rules the last decanate of Sagittarius, whose keyword is *illumination*. Here we find the drive for significance, mapped by the Sun, active as a motivating principle behind actions which lead to or detract from obtaining the just and the true. As symbolized by the white and black sphinxes in the illustration, this drive for self-esteem can be appealed to by both the forces of darkness or the forces of light. Sagittarius tells in esoteric symbology that it is not only when the searching light of the higher mind is used to make a decision that the motivation and assistance of the white forces is assured.

In the Egyptian tarot, Major Arcanum VII is called THE CONQUEROR. At the bottom of the illustration you will note three letters: (1-r) Zayin (Hebrew), Z (English) and Zain (Egyptian). At the top we find the corresponding number to be seven. The Roman numeral VII in the center designates the number of the Major Arcanum. The astrological correspondence of the card is the zodiacal sign of Sagittarius.

A study of the tarot opens wider vistas of astrological interpretation. This Arcanum is a good example of that enlightenment. Sagittarius is the corresponding factor. If we look to the tarot card and then to the constellation which pictures the sign Centaur, we find a fuller meaning. The Centaur draws his bow as far back as possible, showing us combative qualities as well as movement.

Because Sagittarius is a dual sign, it can use either the scepter or the sword. It has natural rule over philosophy, religion, and the higher mind. From the mental angle, the duality is expressed. Mainly, the mental traits express through obedience to those in authority, prompt decision, discipline, and self-control, as well as through a power to command others.

The Conqueror stands in a square-shaped war chariot, which is topped by a starry canopy, drawn over four supporting columns. Across his breast is seen the cuirass, and in each hand he holds a sword and scepter. His crown is mounted with three pentagrams, five-pointed golden stars.

Because he is above the square, it symbolizes his transmutation of the material world with his will power. The four corners of the universe, or quadrants of the heavens surrounding the conqueror are represented by the four columns. They are also associated with the four elemental kingdoms (fire, earth, air, water) which he has mastered with his scepter and sword.

In his right or positive hand he holds aloft the sword, the emblem of physical victory. In his left or negative hand is a scepter topped with a square, a circle, and a triangle. This is universal symbolism which any occult student can discern. The square represents matter and appears at the bottom of the three symbols. A circle symbolizes the realm of the spirit, and the trine stands for the mind. Taken all together these three emblemize a continuous dominion of intelligence over all planes and forces of nature.

At the center front of the chariot we see a spear held by a pair of out-spread wings. It is thus that the immortal flight of the soul through time and endless space is symbolized. As in earlier cards, the sacred serpent appears at the brow, denoting the intellectual light clearly defines fortune and destiny. Three golden pentagrams represent man's control in all three worlds, physical, astral, and spiritual.

The breast plate, or cuirass, represents resistance. On it are pictured a T-square at the bottom and two T-squares above. The Tau, or T-square, appears in many philosophies or orders. It always symbolizes the virile force. You have probably noticed it in symbols of different fraternities, where perhaps even the members do not know its significance.

Above the Tau are two T-squares, representing the just and the true. These are qualities which aid the Conqueror to direct his energies to the right or to the left into mental or physical power whenever it is necessary.

A square-shaped war chariot appears to be drawn by two sphinxes, one white and one black. A sphinx symbolizes the passage of time, as it is composed of the four emblems which correspond to the four zodiacal quadrants, summer, fall, winter, and spring. As white signifies harmony, the white sphinx represents the fortunate periods in time. Black, representing discord, is the color of the sphinx denoting periods of hardship and misfortune. From the esoteric standpoint, these two sphinxes picture the energies which serve the soul in its victorious journey through time, overcoming adversities on the pilgrimage of eternal progression.

In alchemy, Jupiter, the ruler of Sagittarius, corresponds to the metal tin, which has a low melting point. Without tin, or Jupiter, man's life would be stern and severe. In fact, without it there would be little thought given to the welfare of others, and selfishness would dominate all human activities.

The acids of envy and the inroads of remorse can be overcome with the alchemical tin, or Jupiter. To act with true generosity is a far more complex matter than we commonly think it is. It is one thing to be merciful and another just to think of a person's physical needs. Because man is a two-plane organism, assistance, and giving to others should be determined by the use of the higher aspects of mental analysis so that all factors of both the spiritual and material plan can be embraced.

The neophyte who wishes to become a spiritual alchemist should meditate upon the Conqueror. He will learn the value of storing tin in the warehouse of his mind in great abundance. This will attract conditions which can alleviate discordant trends in the environment.

Mentioned in the Bible many times is the chariot. One of the stories relates definitely to Major Arcanum VII, the Conqueror. That is the story of Joseph being sold into Egypt. It is an allegorical tale representing the soul's birth into matter and being chained by primitive and bestial desires.

Upheld in the Conqueror's hand is a sword, indicating Joseph's rise to great power by overcoming all obstacles. The scepter in the Conqueror's left hand indicates that he became an interpreter of the Divine Will because he commanded material forces. Sword is a symbol of physical victory, while the scepter symbolizes mental conquest. This symbolism is well represented in the book *The Sacred Tarot*: "He (Joseph) was tempted by Potiphar's wife, Arcanum VI, but he triumphed (Arcanum VII) over the temptation, even though it meant certain affliction. The dream of Pharaoh which is interpreted of the seven fat kine and the seven lean kine, and the seven good ears and the seven bad ears, related to periods of good and evil, such as the white sphinx and the black sphinx of Arcanum VII signify the result of his triumph through periods of good and periods of evil, and of his not yielding to temptation, is set forth in Gen. 41:41. It is symbolical of what may be expected by others who triumph over temptation; for they also shall be made rulers over the physical plane, which is the land of Egypt.

"And Pharaoh said unto Joseph: See, I have set thee over all the land of Egypt. And Pharaoh took off his ring and put it upon Joseph's hand, and arrayed him in vestures of fine linen, and put a gold chain about his neck; and made him to ride in the second CHARIOT which he had; and they cried before him; Bow the knee; and he made him ruler over all the land of Egypt."

Number seven refers to perfect form on the physical plane. This number is evident in many things, commonly overlooked by the materialist. There are seven tones in the musical scale. There are seven colors in the rainbow. A week is composed of seven days.

The ancients held that we have seven physical senses. They included intuition and though transference to the well-known five.

Seven to the occultist means a yet wider influence. There are seven basic, or so-called lower octave planets used in astrology. They symbolize tools to assist man to overcome the physical plane. Every plane of existence has seven levels. The repeated reference to number seven is to the occultist the key to the pathway of initiation.

Physical initiation of the soul is completed at the seventh step of and unfoldment in the cycle of evolution. Science and magic have been assimilated to the point where the occult powers are enhanced and bring a vibration that is satisfied only when the neophyte is contributing to the cosmic plan.

The temptations of the physical world have been dominated. The neophyte has gained self-mastery. His physical body is under the rule of a disciplined will. His experiences gained in the physical form of the external world have all been met and assimilated.

Vibrating to the same key as Arcanum VII is spiritual astrology. This branch of astrology embraces a knowledge handed down to us from the wisest of all men that tells of the nature of the soul, the destiny of the soul and just what to do about getting on with soul progression.

Using universal symbolism, the sages associated the lessons of life with the starry constellations. They held that God makes known to man his will through a study of the stars. These constellations and the pictured associations give a positive key to the sacred books of the world.

The two keys, one of gold and one of silver, which unlock the secrets and cycles of nature are embraced in astrology and the sacred tarot. The Major Arcana of the tarot hold the keys to soul development and spiritual astrology, giving instructions on how the soul may best go forward in order that it will be able to scale the spiritual heights.

The Conqueror symbolizes the importance of living a spiritual life. The forces and energies of the spirit can be involved to help the soul in its pilgrimage only when motives spring from the realm of the spirit. The spiritual light gives a clearness which banishes the mysteries of life and allows the neophyte to command the land of Egypt, just as the Conqueror did before riding away in his chariot.

Chapter VIII

Importance Of Balance

"Remember, then, son of earth, that to be victorious over thyself and dominate obstacles is but a part of the human task. To accomplish it entirely thou must establish equilibrium between the forces that thou has brought into play. All action produces reaction. The will should foresee the shock of opposite forces in order to temper or annul them. If The Balance should appear in the prophetic signs of thy horoscope, it signifies that the future is balanced between good and evil, and warns that an unbalanced mind is like as abortive Sun."

Major Arcanum VIII, THE BALANCE, is well summed in the foregoing admonition as presented by C.C. Zain. Astrologically, this tarot card corresponds to the zodiacal sign of Capricorn. Thus, if Capricorn is prominent in your horoscope (appearing in the prophetic signs), that admonition is pregnant with meaning. The symbolism pictured on the card broadens the understanding if the neophyte studies and mediates upon it.

In the Egyptian tarot, Major Arcanum VIII is called THE BALANCE. At the bottom of the illustration you will note three letters. (1-r) Cheth (Hebrew), H-CH (English) and Helitha (Egyptian). At the top we find the corresponding number to be eight. The Roman numeral VIII designates the number of the Major Arcanum, and the astrological correspondence is Capricorn.

In adding numbers, there are several combinations which give a sum of eight. Students of numbers find that each combination has a specific function. When eight is composed of two fours, it expresses two opposites, or equilibrium, crystallization, stagnation, and possible death or transition. This expression can manifest on any level. Death, for instance, may refer to the realm of ideas. In its fours aspect, eight is the antithesis of progress, and highly conservative.

As representing man yielding to action, eight is composed of five plus three. Temptation polarized, two plus six. Victory over intelligence and will is represented by seven plus one. Reviewing the tarot card corresponding to these numbers will reveal their full meaning.

Regardless of the components of eight, it is the number of inertia in the macrocosmic realm. As applied to man, it is the number of justice as well as dissolution. Eight comes just before the highest digit of nine, the Diefic number. In the cycle of progression this position is most important.

When THE BALANCE appears in a tarot spread, it may be read as justice and equilibrium. But until the esoteric meaning of the symbolism is understood, this card can be easily misinterpreted.

In the illustration, a blindfolded woman sits upon a throne. She raises a sword in her right hand. A sword is the ancient symbol of justice, weighing all acts and opposing evil. It is the sword of expiration, or purification.

The crown upon the lady's head is made of lance-heads. The lances indicate inflexibility. From her forehead, the sacred serpent with raised head appears signifying that her actions are directed from the realm of the spirit. Above her is a fan of overshadowing protection, symbolizing that justice comes from God.

Scales in her left hand point to the importance of equilibrium between right and duty. Her throne is set upon a platform with three steps, indicating justice in all actions on three planes: Physical, astral, and spiritual. A lion appears on her right side, representing force, and a sphinx, symbolizing the passage of time. It is the controlling of her forces over a period of time which enables her to manifest her best spiritual attributes.

Above and behind her head is a turtle with wings, picturing repentance which brings forgiveness. Then just below the turtle and behind her in a white figure, a divine messenger enwrapping her with protective vibrations. The justice of God will be the final justice of men is what the divine spirit stands for.

A most significant portrayal is the blindfold upon the eyes of justice. At first thought, the import of this symbolism is evasive. But meditation brings the full significance. The eyes are covered to show that justice weights and strikes (the working of immutable law) without thought of petty and conventional difference that men have fashioned for themselves.

We are often told to "fulfill the law" and good will come to us. But this is only half of the story. It is sure that if from dark motivation or from ignorance we fulfill certain laws, no good will come to us. In other words, everything in the universe is under law. Those laws are immutable, unchangeable. Every action taken deals with forces which are under law. Therefore, ignorance is no excuse.

There is a story which illustrates this well. It is one which my late husband used occasionally in his Sunday sermons on the Religion of the Stars. The setting is Miami, just after a refreshing rain storm when the Sun had burst forth and the dew hung heavy and sparkling. During the storm a high-tension pole had been downed. The wires which carry high-voltage electricity had broken, resting upon the pavement about two feet apart. A little girl arrived on the scene to see a beautiful blue light arcing from one wire end to the other. Fascinated, she reached out to touch it. She was electrocuted immediately.

That may not be a pretty story, but it brings home a lesson in a forceful and unforgettable manner. She was not saved by her ignorance. Rather, when she put certain forces into motion, the laws governing those forces were fulfilled and the inevitable resulted. I suggest that you turn back to the admonition that opened this chapter. Perhaps when you read it this time, you will glean a deeper meaning.

It would be quite unfair to leave the subject at that, implying that ignorance is the only sin. Let me offer the following for your consideration.

Immutable law and the secrets of Mother Nature can be unlocked or understood with two keys. The silver key is the tarot, and the golden key is astrology. The tarot synthesizes the Religion of the Stars. Moon rules silver, and Sun rules gold. Coupling of the tarot and astrology is like the New Moon when the Sun and the Moon appear in a conjunction aspect, at the same degree in the zodiac.

Such a phenomena happens about once every lunar month (27.3 days), bringing a fresh impetus to things for growth and expansion. With light comes understanding to enable spiritual progression. Thus an understanding of astrology and the tarot will help us become able to fulfill certain laws which are beneficial.

Arcanum VIII catches the interest of the Bible student. Two

verses from Genesis and one from Revelations point up the weighing of the balance.

Gen. 3:19 we read: ``In the seat of thy face shalt thou eat bread, till thou return into the ground; for out of it wast thou taken, and unto dust shall thou return.'' This passage clearly symbolizes the descent of the spirit through involution into physical matter, and the resultant equilibrium established.

Gen. 19:26: ``But his wife looked back from behind him, and she became a pillar of salt.'' This verse which refers to the selfish motives of Lot's wife, shows what will happen to the neophyte who seeks truth and later returns to his selfish and materialistic ways. From a vibratory standpoint, it means giving up the finer levels which lead to spirituality, and slipping down to a gross vibratory level. Capricorn is the most earthy sign of the zodiac. If the balance is tipped toward materialism, the person attracts discord.

Adding to the interpretation, we find in Rev. 3:16: ``So, then, because thou art lukewarm, and neither cold nor hot, I will spew thee out of my mouth.'' This signifies the polarization of spiritual energies by the grosser animal inclinations.

Matter is spirit in a state of equilibrium. Perfect equilibrium results in crystallization. A physical symbol of this concept is seen when the Sun passes through the zodiacal sign of Capricorn each year. It is then that the waters and vapors of the earth crystalize into ice and snow.

Past experience tells us that there is a tendency for this phenomena to occur annually. Therefore, we can take protective measures against it. It is the same with our spiritual progress. When Capricorn appears in the prophetic signs of a horoscope, experience tells us that certain steps need be taken as symbolized by The Balance in the Egyptian tarot.

Chapter IX

Keys To Self Development

To get the most from the Egyptian tarot, one should have a knowledge of astrology. After the cards are shuffled, cut, and spread, then this knowledge comes to the aid of the reader.

To demonstrate how through association astrology assists in the interpretation of the cards, let us look at Aquarius, the zodiacal sign which corresponds to Arcanum IX.

Aquarius, the eleventh sign of the zodiac, is the Man. Belonging to the air element, Aquarius depicts a love of society and stimulation through the interchange of mental conceptions. Although it is a fixed sign, its airy quality gives a certain continuity. External environment plays an important role as a stimulus to behavior.

Being a masculine sign, assertiveness comes to the fore. People with a strong Aquarian accent in their horoscopes are progressive, friendly, scientific, have a pleasant manner. They are usually influenced by kindness, have an artistic trend and due to their strong likes and dislikes they love to argue. Their interest follows lines on the mental level, especially in new and progressive things.

Should Arcanum IX appear in a spread which has to do with some associate, just the brief description above will give a fund of information about him: His temperament, how best to approach him, as well as his manner of doing things and his motive.

Perhaps another reading concerns the self development of the querent. When Arcanum IX turns up, here is a key to things which can help his development on any plane. If the question is about spiritual matters, then a knowledge of the alchemy associated with the sign will reveal correct steps to be taken. Nature furnishes all of us with impure metals. It is our job to transmute them. Tools which help us in this endeavor are capacity and ability.

These tools are shown in a birth chart or in the symbolism of the tarot spread. Both astrology and the tarot point the way toward the selection of thoughts, feelings, and actions which will attract the events and opportunities that help us in our development on all levels, spiritual, mental, emotional, and physical.

In the spiritual realm Aquarius expresses as absolute wisdom. Intellectually, it is associated with the direction of the will. On the physical level, it designates precautionary actions as a guide to behavior.

As with all other things in nature, Aquarius is seen from two sides. When the energies it pictures are being expressed in a constructive manner, altruistic trends come out. There is a great concern about things from the standpoint of the welfare of society at large. Thus, if an Aquarian card, major or minor, turns right side up, these trends can be considered.

However, if the card is reversed, then the other manifestation of energies under this air sign have a tendency to express in argumentation. Attention in this case is shifted to self as the one who knows all. Argument just for the sake of argument, no constructive motive, replaces the higher expression of altruism. Interpreted in this manner the card is a clue to the kind of person one will deal with in regards to the things asked about.

Self development demands the use of spiritual alchemy. When an alchemical process, no matter what kind, is adopted, there is a danger present if matters are forced. The raising of energies expressing habitually on an inharmonious level to an expression on a constructive level is called transmutation. Time should be allowed for a successful demonstration, because transmutation does not take effect immediately. Forcing the process by trying to alter conditions too speedily can bring drastic results.

Whenever energies need transmuting (a horoscope or a tarot spread point them out) they should be handled by gradually directing them into channels that lead to the sought-for goal of expression. Undue haste and restless impatience are the greatest blocks to successful transmutation. The Sage, Arcanum IX, depicts the qualities which alone enable the alchemist to attain success. Briefly, this card is read as wisdom or prudence.

Most astrologers and taroists will agree that to be most successful in helping self and others to develop by using the horoscope or the tarot cards, the reader should be well versed in psychology. From this angle, the mental factors associated with Uranus and Aquarius mold the channel through which the actual words of the reading are given, that is if these points are prominent in a chart or spread.

In the case of the Aquarian mind, there is great activity and a constant flux of subject matter. For a while the old way is well and good, but soon ideas for new ways enter the mind. It is this progressive trend which gives the ingenious inventiveness to the Aquarian. In fact, such replacing of the old with the new is one of the foundations of survival. Self-preservation and race preservation, which demand the adaptation to an ever changing environment, are naturally benefitted as a result of a better approach. Mental elements and conceptions under this sign are many times responsible for the beneficial and progressive trends in society.

In a reading, insight into the person, object or thing asked about is keyed by the astrological symbolism. All other signs, planets, and the zodiacal decanates give clues which when viewed from the broad scope of what is behind astrological hieroglyphs broadens and deepens any tarot or astrological reading.

Major Arcanum IX is called THE SAGE. The three letters at the bottom of the illustration are (1-r) Teth (Hebrew), TH (English) and Thela (Egyptian). At the top we find the corresponding number to be nine. The Roman numeral designates the number of the Major Arcanum of the tarot. The numerical correspondence of the card is the zodiacal sign of Aquarius.

The highest digit, nine, is the Diefic number. It is a most interesting number. It can be multiplied by any number, and when the digits of the result of the multiplication are added crosswise, they will always resolve into nine.

Seven is the number of the physical plane, and evidence is seen on every hand. There are seven colors of the spectrum, or seven tones of the musical scale. It is claimed that the astral realms, or those frequencies which dominate the four-dimensional realms, are scaled to the number nine. In addition, where physical vibratory rates are measured in octaves, their astral counterparts are scaled in decaves.

Nine is the symbol of manifested Diety, all the expressions of which can be reduced back to first matter, or the primal source. In this aspect, nine is the digit which unlocks the cycles of the ancients.

Esoteric lessons of the ancients are presented in the picture of The Sage. He is an old wanderer, leaning on a staff, carrying a light which is half concealed by his mantle. He symbolizes experience gained along the pathway of life. The ancients used the square to represent the physical world. His mantle is square in form, meaning that the physical world is the plane where man can gain knowledge of good and evil.

To show that The Sage has acquired this knowledge, his cape (physical limitations) is partially removed as he beams the rays of the lamp (intelligence) over the past, present, and future. Note that the lamp is partially hidden in his mantle, showing discretion. In other words, if the real nature of anything (the truth) is to be known, a delving beneath external appearance is necessary.

A staff in his right hand signifies that man evolves through friction and struggle; first overcoming obstacles and then being engulfed by them. Finally the realization comes to him that only through transmuting the lower expressions of his inherent energies through overcoming obstacles on life's pathway will his staff of prudence give him spiritual security in all of his activities.

Wisdom that is represented by The Sage comes from within and without. The ancients presented this concept both in the two serpents which appear in his headdress, and those at his feet. Experience with good and evil is the result of impressions and reactions gained in the inner realms.

These two factors of knowledge are symbolized by the hieroglyph (the two way lines) we use to represent the sign Aquarius. The Sage has sat at the feet of external teachers. He has also been guided by those occupying the inner planes of life.

Each soul in the universe was brought forth to fulfill a cosmic mission. The promptings which urge a conservation for self development derive from the Divine Spark within each of us. At any new point in consciousness, each soul has a task through which he may contribute to cosmic welfare.

Upon each soul's faithfulness in performing whatever is placed in his hands to do at anytime, depends his future opportunities for progression. Therefore, self development is of great import. A splendid way to assist in the Great Work is to employ astrology and the tarot. They unlock the keys to self development.

Chapter X

Change And Destiny

A phone call came from a reader asking if I believed in serpent worship. This question surprised me. I wondered what she meant by serpent worship and why she thought I believed in it. On second thought I realized that in my writings on the Egyptian tarot the serpent was featured several times in the symbolism used to portray the ancient teachings.

In order to perpetuate esoteric teachings, the ancient masons traced the symbolism on the tarot plates. These symbolical photographs set forth in most complete detail how the signs of the zodiac and the planets in the sky influence human life and destiny.

These sages can be traced back to the early inhabitants of the valley of the Tigris and Euphrates. Going back still further, evidences of this esoteric knowledge have been found in the seven ancient centers of civilization: Egypt, India, Crete, Peru, China, Mexico, and Chaldea.

Because these ideas were identical in spite of the varied presentations by these peoples in the widely scattered centers, it is reasonable to suppose that they had their origin in the same place. The two now sunken islands, Atlantis in the Atlantic and Mu in the Pacific, had both attained an extremely high scientific culture which included the Secret Doctrine. The colonists who escaped before the lands were submerged brought the spiritual ideas to the seven ancient centers mentioned above.

To portray certain spiritual concepts, the seers of old used the symbol of the serpent along with that of the Sun and other pictographs. The life-giving qualities of the Sun and the reproductive powers of the serpent were merely symbols used by the ancient masons to convey the Great Truths to the populace. Because of its wave-like motion of travel, its coiling, and its phallic significance, the snake has been used throughout the world as the glyph of verile power and creative energy. Hence

it came to be the emblem of the sun, the source of such creative energy.

In ancient times, as in some instances today, certain groups, instead of recognizing the serpent and the Sun as esoteric symbols, endowed them both with divine qualities. Such groups set the Sun and the serpent as objects of worship.

To make clear the use of the serpent in symbology in the Egyptian tarot, it might be well to state now that the serpent represents creative energy. When the head of the serpent is lifted, a constructive use of the creative energies is indicated. However, should the serpent be pictured with its head down or in a low position, the creative energies are dissipated in a slough of destruction.

A serpent can be seen on Major Arcanum X which is called THE WHEEL. The three letters at the bottom of the illustration are (1-r) Jod (Hebrew), I, J, Y (English) and Ioothi (Egyptian). At the top we find the corresponding number to be 10. The Roman numeral X designates the number of the Major Arcanum. The astrological correspondence of the card is the planet Uranus.

If the tarot reader is well versed in astrology he can give a splendid reading of this card, because there is a natural affinity. The occult science associated with this card is natal astrology. Before explaining the correspondence, it might be well to explain the symbolism used here.

First glance shows a wheel of spokes attached to a dual column. The taroist calls this the wheel of destiny. On the right side of the wheel we see Hernanubis, the genius of good. He is trying to mount to the peak of the wheel. On the left side we find Typhon, the genius of evil. The eight spokes of the wheel represents justice (see Arcanum VIII). This pictures that in the course of Divine Providence time and opportunity are meted out to all in a just and fair manner.

At the top poised on a circular platform balancing on the wheel is a sphinx holding a javelin in its claws. This signifies that time is ever stimulating events and always ready to strike to right or left, as the wheel of destiny springs under its impetus. The entire ensemble portrays the raising of the humble and the lowering of the proud.

The dual column from which the wheel is suspended symbolizes that all nature expresses is polarity, positive and negative. Because all action is the result of this polarity (sex) a serpent was drawn by the ancient Masons on the spokes of the wheel. At the foot of this dual column there are two more serpents with heads raised to indicate that a spiritual attitude brings change to a new and higher field of endeavor. When reading cards, Arcanum X may be read as change of fortune.

Reviewing this symbology, it will be easier to understand the significance of esoteric astrology and the tarot. Uranus is the higher octave expression of Mercury. In the tarot, Arcanum X (Uranus) is the second decave of Arcanum I (Mercury). It takes Uranus about seven years to travel through one sign of the zodiac. To pass through the 12 houses of the horoscope completing the whole circle of the zodiac, it takes 84 years.

A complete cycle of Uranus coincides with the present life span of man. It corresponds to the idealistic perfection in each department of life as represented by the houses of the horoscope.

Uranus is the planet which more than any other is associated with abrupt changes of fortune, good or evil. Trends of unexpected change also manifest in the mental viewpoint. Astrologers have found that people with a prominent Uranus in their horoscopes have lightning like minds. They seem to take short-cuts when using their reasoning powers.

Psychologically, the predominately Aquarian mind is an interesting study. Instead of the slow, laborious workings of the objective mind, the reasoning process is carried out in the subconscious mind where more complete data is available and where conclusions are drawn immediately. There these conclusions impress the objective consciousness as intuition.

When we first look at number 10, we are impressed with the appearance of the numerals which compose it. There are two digits: one and zero. No Arabic numerals are more truly symbolic than these two. One appears at one end of a series and the other ending and starting a new series of numbers. Nothing is more obvious as a symbol for unity than is a short, straight line. All is contained in one, and it is potential undeveloped. With the symbol 10, the source of which is the same as the Sun, all potentials are manifesting to complete one series. The two numerals taken together represent a cycle. The straight line is positive, and the circle is negative. Ten is the completion of one cycle and the beginning of another. When one cycle ends, another arises out of it; there is a union of forces. A change from the old order is seen when a transition to a new phase or order of existence takes place.

Many examples from the Bible might be cited to show an early knowledge of the Sacred Tarot upon the part of the Hebrews. However, their later writings, with a few exceptions, do not contain much of it. Daniel seems to have had some knowledge of applying the silver key, as the tarot is called. The whole of the apocalypse is based upon the tarot. A survey of this literature tends to show that at the death of David such information was lost to the Jewish priesthood.

Later there is evidence to show that inspired prophets recovered it. Aside from the Bible, other sacred writings of ancient nations can be interpreted more fully by the tarot. As Eliphas Levi said: "Without the tarot, the magi of the ancients is a closed book, and it is impossible to penetrate any of the great mysteries of the Kabala."

By the tarot alone can the mystic symbology of Ezekiel's writings be intelligently interpreted. Arcanum X portrays the Wheel of Ezekiel, referred to in Chapter 1, Verse 15: "Now, as I beheld the living creatures, behold, one wheel upon the earth by the living crates, with is four faces."

He was referring to the composite symbols embraced in the sphinx: the lion, the bull, the eagle and the Man. The golden key of astrology ties in here, because the four fixed signs of the zodiac are mentioned. An interpretation of the four-fold Sphinx can be stated in terms of universal principles. That is, all life, action, and progress results from interacting forces. This signifies change and the wheel of fortune.

There is a basic formula underlying all manifestation. (1)A positive force and (2)a negative force (3)unite, producing a (4)certain result. Or, to state it another way: The energy of the lion (Leo) expresses through the sex of the eagle (Scorpio) bringing about material incarnation and the plodding toil of the bull (Taurus), to the end of evolving the immortal man (Aquarius). In Ezek, 1:13, the two figures on the wheel of Arcanum X are mentioned: "As for the likeness of the living creatures, their appearance was like burning coals of fire, and like the appearance of lamps; it went up and down amid the living creatures and the fire was bright and out of the fire was lightening."

The Arcanum which is associated with Uranus depicts sudden and unexpected changes on all plans. One cycle is completed and a new one emerges. Other interesting Biblical stories illustrating the change of fortune will be found in the lives of Solomon and Zadekiah.

Chapter XI

The Touchstone Of Purity

Major Arcanum XI of the tarot series not only symbolizes the necessity of transmuting energies, it gives the method of doing so. Keying this concept is the enchanting and dramatic Neptune.

Divination is the occult science associated with this card. The foreknowledge of future trends, divination is a valuable tool to be used in the art of creative living. Every life presents opportunities that allow a person to create better conditions for himself. Day after day, week after week, each soul is called upon to face life's ever-changing conditions. Each person's attitude of mind determines just what adjective he would use to describe the kaleidoscopic patterns of living.

One type may say his life is filled with sorrows and troubles. Usually he does all he can to demonstrate a more troublesome and sorrowful condition. Then there is the type who says life presents many problems; but the problems are a challenge, because if they are true ones, they have a solution. This approach to living is more constructive than the former. A third type sets a sparkling example for all.

"Creative imagination" is not some complicated, formidable, mysterious something to the third type. He grasps every opportunity to exercise his creative abilities. Maybe you think that washing dishes or watering the lawn is not creative. Mundane stuff? Did you ever stop to realize that the very action taken is the result of a mental process? Action stems from mental stimulation. Arcanum XI represents that story.

Neptune is the idealist. But when the iridescence of promising rainbows is captured and directed to the material plane, we join the best of the ideal and material, the offspring of which is the ultimate creative expression in this earthly life.

Major Arcanum XI is called THE ENCHANTRESS. The three letters at the bottom of the illustration are (1-r) Caph (Hebrew), C-K (English), and Caitha

(Egyptian). At the top we find the corresponding number to be 11. The Roman numeral XI designates the number of the Major Arcanum of the Egyptian tarot. The astrological correspondence of the card is the planet Neptune.

In reading a tarot spread, Arcanum XI is keyed by the words, "Force, Spiritual Power, or Fortitude." As with the other 77 tarot cards, the key is just a starting point. An opening wedge for the subconscious mind, as it were. A proficient reader is usually well versed in astrology and the philosophy of the tarot.

After reading the conventional keyword of the card, the subconscious mind is stimulated and reveals information from the storehouse of knowledge by which symbolism is expanded in its interpretation to cover a vast concept of what a particular card means in relation to the matter asked about.

There is a wealth of esoteric meaning behind the number 11. In the study of Arcanum X as composed of two fives, the Cosmic man, or humanity, we find both man and woman. Ten shows they are both active in a new and higher field of endeavor, because 10 represents the completed cycle as well as the starting point of another cycle. However, the numerical significance of the number 11 points to the forces of nature that are magnetic and feminine. Regardless of various opinions prevalent today, woman molds the efforts of man through his affectionate nature. Although the finer forces of woman do not give actual physical strength to man, they appeal to his positive, innate nature. Like the Enchantress, she enters his life in a subtle manner, feeling the flaming spirit which rests inert in the womb of his genius. The finer feminine forces that awaken the latent powers within him act as a touchstone, releasing his highest ideals.

Symbolically, Arcanum XI represents the power that can be developed and used to counteract violent forces of nature. Prerequisites to development include self-confidence, or faith in self, as well as living the life of the spirit.

Spiritual power is the natural result following actions which dominate and rule the animal instincts. Through the use of directed thinking and induced emotions, purer affections predominate. This purity is the touchstone. Rather than avoiding it, evil should be overcome by goodness, for power stems from goodness alone.

Outstanding in the illustration are the maid and the lion. Her hands are pictured on jaws of the angry beast. She opens and closes his mouth without effort. On her head is a crown upon which rests a vase and a crowned eagle.

At her brow is the sacred serpent, telling in pictorial language that she does not act blindly. She is keenly aware of the vibrant power within her. She knows exactly how to utilize it for the greater benefit of others. The vase stands for the affections which, when transmuted to finer vibratory rates, soar to the greatest heights, tasting deeply of lofty aspirations. The crowned eagle was used by the ancient masons to depict this spiritual force.

In contrast, the lion appears in the lower position. It was used to symbolize these same forces expressing on a lower plane, as well as to portray the animal desires in man. A sweeping glance from the bottom to the top reveals the concept that gross desires have been subdued and transformed by the spiritual nature.

To have meaning in our daily lives, the symbolic ensemble should be associated with the things which weave the pattern of existence. It is well and good to say the lower desires should be transmuted, but in coming to grips with the work involved, that simple statement leads to many complexities.

A general approach can be taken if we think of the Enchantress as the positive or constructive side of ourselves, while the lies, the tempting desires keyed on a lower scale within our minds. One is positive, and one is negative. To attain the significance of number 11, which is the balancing of forces with the use of the magnetic principle, we should so live our lives so that we can use this basic law of the universe to build up within ourselves a more refined and spiritual vibratory rate.

The ancient masons conveyed the importance of lifting the self up and up to become a more efficient part of the Divine Plan. They also give the keys to how it can be done in the illustration of Arcanum XI. It is extremely rewarding to sit in meditation with this picture as the subject of concentration. Avenues to the inner treasures of wisdom open and lead the seeker to places which, though corresponding to Neptune, have a practical application as well as the pleasing and enjoyable feeling of the expansive planet.

A scrutinizing look at daily life reveals that creative imagination, as ruled by Neptune, plays an important part in attracting what comes to us. Some immediately think of famous objects when they think of creative imagination; for instance, Roden's "Thinker," DaVinci's "Mona Lisa," or one of the Schubert Serenades. Certainly all took a Neptunian stimulus, but this same stimulation is experienced many times by all of us. Yet, not all of us have the potential of a Roden or a DaVinci. However, we do have the environment at all times in which we can use some of the stuff of the Enchantress to create newer and better conditions for ourselves and those around us. Life itself is a greater art than all the so-called arts put together. If a person has missed this intriguing concept, he is not using all possible combinations of hues on the pallet from which he paints the picture of his own life.

If full intellectual and emotional realization of the symbolic message of Arcanum XI comes to us, we have assimilated a valuable spiritual fact. The principles of creative imagination will be used unconsciously, just as doing the dishes or watering the lawn, after a period of practice. We can apply them to every department of life as represented by the mundane houses of the birth chart. Among other things these include self improvement, financial security, marriage and family relations, the home, any type of work undertaken, parenthood, relations with friends, and the multitude of other areas in our daily lives.

In a general way, these principles applied daily in whatever environment we are, from home to school to the office, bring in rewarding results. But the supreme results come to him who has a guide of his own inner being. The most reliable one will be found in his individual horoscope, which has been calculated for the date, place, and hour of birth.

Using the patterns pictured in the horoscope, he has the power to lift the most commonplace events of daily life from drudging routine into a creative masterpiece as he wields his brush (subconscious mind) to paint a self-portrait of his life.

Here is an interesting and fruitful experiment for anyone with his own horoscope and some astrological knowledge. Place Arcanum XI in the position of Neptune in the birth chart. Then read the following admonition by C.C. Zain. Even though the words will be the same for each horoscope, there can be no two alike. The particular planetary patterns and positions of each chart lend a special interpretation: "Remember, then, son of earth, that for power one must believe in one's ability. Advance with faith. To become strong, impose silence upon the weakness of the heart. If Arcanum XI should appear in the prophetic signs of thy horoscope, thou shouldst study duty, which is the rule of right, and practice justice as if you loved it."

In astrology, Neptune is the higher octave expression of Venus. Both planets refer to the affections. Yet there is a vast difference between the basic thought of the two, even though it is necessary to understand and utilize the forces represented by both planets in order to tap the highest manifestations of either one alone. Venus is associated with material love as distinct from the spiritual love of Neptune.

A prominent Neptune in a horoscope shows a tendency for psychic ability, and being a higher octave planet, it seldom expresses on outer environment directly. Rather, its stimulation coincides with activity in the minds of people, and it plays an important role in the process of imagination. Because of a great sensitivity that usually comes with the development of qualities under Neptune's rulership, the faith angle given in the admonition is important.

Positive faith balances the negativeness, and this coupling process used by occultists in a constructive manner is the concept the ancient masons wished to convey in the illustration of Arcanum XI. Some of the forces involved are extremely subtle. Thus, if the positiveness is not encouraged while inducing creative imagination, facets of information may be entirely overlooked. Information which could be helpful or harmful, as the case may be. This is so because the thought-forms generated are not forceful, as in the case of demonstrating under an aggressive Mars stimulus.

A quick recap of the plays you have seen, the books you have read, or the experiences you have heard about from others, gives an impression that unhappiness and obstacles are the elements of drama. It may seem more dramatic to suffer, but if we face the dweller on the threshold, face true spiritual values, we do not have to admit the basic reason for the assumption. In being thwarted and unhappy we give ourselves an opening to comfort and cuddle our weak spots with self-pity. This, in spite of the fact that within our higher self resides the principles of universal truth that tell us the quality of self-pity is one of the most destructive emotions that man can hold. Self-pity is soul poisoning.

If an attitude is held for a period of time, it determines the habitual vibratory level of a person's expression. Thus if we dramatize through self-pity, it goes without saying that we are demonstrating downward on the scale of spirituality.

Arcanum XI with its spiritual lesson gives us information which we can apply daily in order to avoid retrogression. If we face each day with a determination to practice the concept symbolized by the lion and the maid, we can change this dull and tiresome personality into a vibrant, pleasurable expression by the constructive use of creative imagination. The keywords are: Force, spiritual power or fortitude.

Chapter XII

Above And Beyond Belief

Pisces, the last sign of the zodiac, naturally associated with the twelfth house of the horoscope, is the astrological correspondence of Major Arcanum XII in the Egyptian tarot. Other things which fall naturally under this rulership are crime, expiration, sacrifice, and disappointments. It sounds like a neatly tied bundle of negativism, doesn't it?

A dual sign, Pisces the emotional water sign, also corresponds to a potently high expression. The Hanged Man in the tarot tells of the inevitable results when the neophyte does not strive for this constructive expression of the energies pictured.

In the illustration the three letters at the bottom are (1-r) Lamed (Hebrew), L (English), and Luzian (Egyptian). At the top we find the corresponding number to be 12. The Roman numeral XII designates the number of the Major Arcanum, and the symbol of Pisces gives the astrological association.

A gallows, from which a man is suspended, is supported by two trees, each having six cut branches. The 12 cut branches were used by the ancient masons to indicate the destruction of the twelve houses of the horoscope. It was in this manner that they told of the extinction of life from the spiritual plane unless the energies which play upon the soul were utilized for constructive endeavor. The mending of the cut branches insured the building of a sound spiritual body.

Recently, I saw a cartoon in a juvenile Sunday school paper which was pertinent to the idea expressed here. A rugged fruit tree was pictured, from which grew branches with lush green leaves and fruit bursting with ripeness. Here and there could be seen dead limbs with dried and shriveled leaves. A pair of hands holding pruning shears was busy cutting out the dead branches, which were appropriately labeled temper, indifference, selfishness, pride and self-glory.

The caption read, "They who bear fruit must bear pruning." The Bible reference was John 15:2. Any gardener knows the secret of keeping planets and trees pruned so that all the nourishment will go to the developing fruit or flower. So it is with our spiritual growth. If we prune out the limbs of negativism, then all of our vital energy will flow into constructive channels. This is a process which is necessary to build a spiritual body.

The Hanged Man's position gives two significant symbols: The tied hands pointing downward for a triangle, and the crossing of one leg over the other knee forms a cross. This relationship shows the cross above the triangle, indicating that material forces, passion, and lust have gained the center of attention, while the mind has been left neglected far into the background.

From his tied hands, coins are seen dropping to earth. Because the approach taken is stamped with materialism, these dropping coins show that much effort is wasted and that life's forces are dissipated. Just as a coin has two sides unalike, the ancient ones told a dual story in this symbolism. This is a sign of violent and unexpected death, but at the same time with a different and higher motivation, it also represents the expiration of crime, and even death accepted voluntarily through heroic devotion to truth and justice.

In addition, the dropping coins symbolize that the martyr's efforts are never lost when he loses his life in furthering truth and justice. The results of his efforts remain on earth after he passes. When a man steps out of the conventional pattern to progress he inevitably goes through self-sacrifice. Look at the ridicule that was thrown down on Louis Pasteur when he first presented the proof of bacteria in certain diseases. Then there was Galileo, who was persecuted when he told of the discoveries of his telescope. So it goes throughout the ages. The people who have given mankind its greatest blessings have found themselves flirting with punishment, all because they departed too far from current belief.

Pisces action stems from the phrase "I believe." There is a passive acceptance, as a rule, unless a conscious effort is made to practice intellectual discrimination. The latter can be accomplished easily under the Piscean influence, if we make a determined effort to use the impressionable and psychic side of the sign in our search for reality. Pisces is associated with the proverbial "pink clouds," "bubbles," and "illusion." If this is recognized at the start, there is a powerful possibility to cast aside these nebulous traits and get at the core of truth. Students of esoteric symbolism think of "the rock" in association with the word "truth." Peter, of the New Testament, means "rock." If you remember that Bible story, you will recall that Peter was commanded to found his church upon a rock (truth). All of the import pointing to constructive endeavor is symbolized by Peter. The keys to understanding are not symbolized in the conventional manner in his hand. They are represented by a seven-pointed crown on his head. The use of intellect is shown by his head, end the seven points refer to the septenary (lower octave) planets, or astrology. If the intellect is called into play to direct astrological energies, then comes understanding (Pisces rules the feet) of truth.

In order to become useful, these mystical stories should be interpreted on the practical plane. After all, each thought, feeling and action we have today is building for our tomorrows, whether they be here or hereafter. Because this is a fact of eternal life, its consideration is most important to all living persons. Unless we consider the factors of the physical world, as well as those of the astral world, we can not expect to understand the whole truth.

Pisces rules the natural twelfth house of the horoscope. It is also associated with the energies that influence our thinking in a most subtle manner, energies which come from unseen sources. It, more than any other sign of the zodiac, probably pictures the large number of minds today. Blind belief is prevalent. This is not too surprising when we consider that all evolution for the past 2000 years has been polarized in the so-called Piscean Age. It was a period of development in the eternal cycle of progression. But now with the dawning age of Aquarius, these Piscean approaches should be reexamined and redirected, so that they will find a constructive place in the Divine Pattern.

James Harvey Robinson, historian and social scientist, once discussed two telling words. They had to do with *reasons*. In appropriate stories during his lectures, he brought out the difference between "good" and "real" reasons. A *good* reason for doing something would be satisfactory to the Pisces mind. But the Aquarius mind needs a *real* reason for action. This duality is pictured in the Major Arcanum XII. If we believe only and let "good" reasons shape our choices, we might end up like the hanged man. However, if intellect is applied and the higher side of the Pisces nature is allowed to express, we build for spirituality, thus avoiding the hanging.

Subtleties have a great influence on our ideas, opinions and preferences. Did you ever stop to consider the *real* reasons why you belong to the clubs you do, the church you do, and the *real* reasons why you accept astrology and other occult sciences? You can probably give a *good* reason for every one of your answers, but the *real* reason is something else again. Just as the Pisces influence is secret and subtle, the real reasons for our beliefs are concealed.

In most cases, children are not taught to do their own thinking. Most of us, when faced with the truth of our development, would have to admit that our ideas have been absorbed from the environment about us rather than being adopted from the result of analytical thinking. If we find ourselves living a life that does not offer all we think it should (some call it a state of unhappiness) then it would seem the first step to cure the social ill would be to bring the searchlight of analysis upon all our thoughts, feelings, and actions.

It is through our thoughts, feelings, and actions that we shape our lives. Therefore, if life is not what we think it should be, we should go about changing our thoughts, feelings, and actions. Or to put it in the terms of the pictured Arcanum, it is time to prune the deadwood and mend the broken branches.

A critical examination of our ideas, beliefs, and opinions is a good step in the right direction. Such analysis usually shows that changes need to be made. Change is the watchword of progression. Being a mutable sign, Pisces can adjust to change when a determined effort is made to hold a steady course. Sacrifice, a word often associated with this twelfth sign of the zodiac, can be more completely understood, when constructive change is used as a synonym.

From an idealistic standpoint the sacrifice of the animal part of our nature upon an altar representing devotion to universal welfare, is in reality beneficial. We gain through such sacrifice, because the very frequencies of thought which prompt and sustain such an idea build a spiritual body. In adding and keeping such exalted vibrations, we become a broadcaster of radiations which emanate from us to assist others, and at the same time attract things - both on the physical as well as the inner plane - which provide us the opportunities to be "happy." A two-fold approach is a must in the cosmic scheme of things. To have all the material things one would desire and no spirituality results in a restlessness that stirs discontent within. Conversely, to polarize all the attention on the things of the inner plane, without applying them to the physical plane, usually leads to various degrees of obsession. In this business of living, a balance of the knowledge gained from both planes gives the most satisfactory result.

The dual rulership of Pisces (Neptune's idealism and Jupiter's faith) needs to be tempered with discrimination. If such a state is established, then the subtle influences, both good and bad, which come abundantly through this psychic sign can be handled in a constructive manner. Bringing the intellect to bear on problems of life insures a better fate than that of the man on Arcanum XII. But believe alone, and be hanged.

Chapter XIII

Aquarian Age Conditions

During the Aquarian Age many truths will unfold and become widely accepted. Perhaps one of the greatest truths will concern life after death, the nature of that life and the establishment of communication between the two planes of life.

Many people will come to grasp the conditions of that life in rather minute detail, even before their transition. They will come to realize that pleasure and pain, success and failure also express in the future life. A revelation which should spur them into action to prepare for a future existence while yet here on earth.

Such an understanding will no doubt cause people to open their consciousness to higher levels, learning best how to train themselves while still here on earth in order that they be better fitted to face their eventual responsibilities in that life to come.

Then when enough peoples of the earth are living a completely constructive life here and now, conditions will prevail to make possible the establishment of a non-restricted system of communication between peoples who live and act on the different planes of life.

Aquarius, the eleventh sign of the zodiac, corresponds to the constellation Aquarius, the place in which we now find the Vernal Equinox. The symbolical pictograph used by the ancient masons for this eleventh sign of the zodiac portrays much. A man is holding a gauge in his left, or receptive, hand and an urn in his right hand. His left hand measures the influence of the heaven by means of a 24-hour gauge, while his right, or active, hand holds the urn from which pours down all of the wisdom he has gained.

Man will come of age in Aquarius. This is the concept held by the masters and teachers through the ages. Though there is considerable argument as to the commencement of the Aquarius Age, undoubtedly most will agree that we have recently, or will in the near future, enter this cosmic cycle.

The argument as to the precise time of the event stems from the fact that there is not undisputed record of the date when the first of Aries among the constellations (irregular groups of stars in outer space) coincided with the first of Aries among the zodiacal signs (the 12 equal segments of the heavens).

Today, we cannot with certainty select the western boundary of the constellation of Aries, because just where the precise boundary should be is unknown. Then, too, it is not known whether the picture that appears on today's maps is the same size and shape as that of the ancients.

Due to these factors, there is no exact astronomical observation to tell exactly when the Aquarian Age began. After years of research, C.C. Zain established a time which apparently ties in with the things activated under Aquarius. The date he used for the commencement of the Aquarian Age in his research is January 19, 1881. The Aquarian Age horoscope for this date can be found in *Astrology: 30 years Research*.

His research was carried on in much the same way as that employed in rectifying a birth chart. A time limit was picked within which most considerations (astronomical, mathematical, and sociological) seemed reasonable. Then a chart was chosen through trial and error that clearly indicated events which were not of the type characteristic of Pisces, the preceding age.

History written since 1881 is fairly recent and known to follow a pattern which seems to tie in well with the sign of the zodiac, Aquarius, and the ruler, Uranus. Invention, psychology, electricity, and astronomy, among other things, come under the astrological signature of Uranus. In this period of time since 1881, the world has adopted electricity as its important source of power; industry has been revolutionized by invention; astronomy has extended its boundaries beyond our solar system to other universes. All of the Uranian activities have come about in the fairly recent past.

The pattern of human conduct is formed by religion. Religion, even more than industrial and scientific progress, is showing the impress of a new cosmic trend. Science, by itself, because it embraces classified information, gives a power to do things. Science unveiled atomic fission. Yet, whether the power is used to benefit or to subjugate mankind is a religious consideration. How will man, whose conduct is formed by religion, use atomic power? Atomic bombs or atomic-powered submarines, such as the Nautilus, can be used for constructive purposes or destructive purposes.

Aquarius, a double-rulership sign of the zodiac, has for a symbol two wavy lines. It is a dual sign likened to alternating electricity. Saturn and Uranus are the rulers. Saturn is associated with selfishness or poverty on one hand, or planned conservation on the other, while Uranus is associated with the uninhibited radical, or progressive humanitarian endeavor.

Attitude determines whether Saturn selfishness will hold sway, or if the finer side of Aquarius will be reflected in a humanitarian spirit. This idea follows the ancient kaballistical quote: "As above, so below." True, the world is a whole in itself under the influence of the Aquarian Age, but each of us also has a part of the whole within us.

Each person on earth is a cell within the body of the cosmic man. As each improves his spirituality, so the whole progresses. The Aquarian Age finds each soul at a point in evolution where, to survive and accomplish its Divine mission, he must understand the concepts of THE REAPER, or Arcanum XIII of the sacred tarot, the bible of the Aquarian Age.

Major Arcanum XIII is called THE REAPER. The three letters at the bottom of the illustration are (1-r) Mem (Hebrew), M (English) and Matalch (Egyptian). At the top we find the corresponding number to be 13. The Roman numeral XIII designated the number of the Major Arcanum of the Egyptian tarot. The astrological correspondence of the card is the zodiacal sign Aries.

Each of the Major Arcanum of the tarot can be interpreted in three worlds: spiritual, intellectual, and physical. If the three-fold expression of each of the 22 Major Arcana is assimilated, the neophyte can find the concepts of the Aquarian religion.

Take the Reaper. In the spiritual world, it corresponds to the continuous motion of creation. We might dub it cosmic metabolism, for it involves destruction and renewal. Transformation takes place in both substance and form. A death of the old comes with the production of the new and more refined. Transmutation takes place.

On the intellectual level, the Reaper expresses as the spirit ascending to divine spheres. Individual consciousness seeks the highest level possible to insure it obeys the mandates of the Supreme Intelligence.

In the physical world, the Reaper expresses as death. The soul leaves the physical body to live in an astral body in the astral world.

Blending the three expressions gives an integrated picture of the true significance of transition, so-called death. The idea is excellently expressed by C.C. Zain.

"Remember, then, son of the earth, that terrestrial things are of short duration and that the highest powers are reaped as the grass of the field. If Arcanum XIII should appear in the prophetic signs of thy horoscope, the dissolution of thy organs will come sooner than thou expectest. But do not dread it, for death is but the parturition of another life. The universe reabsorbs without ceasing all which springs from her bosom that has not spiritualized itself. But the releasing of ourselves from material instincts by a free and voluntary adhesion of our souls to the law of universal movement constitutes in us the creation of a second man, a celestial man, and begins our immortality."

In the colored version of Arcanum XIII, the detailed symbolism becomes more apparent than can be seen in the black and white reproduction presented here. A skeleton, or Time, is reaping human heads, hands, and feet. On the blade of the scythe he uses there is a serpent and a scarab. The serpent depicts the energy which urges the soul, symbolized by the scarab, on its evolutionary journey, or incarnating into more and more complex bodies.

The progression of the scythe in the work emblemizes the perpetual destruction and rebirth of all forms of life as time goes by. The mowing of human hands, heads, and feet symbolizes man's thoughts, works, and understanding will finally pass from earth. Behind all is seen a rainbow in the sky, promising a new life of thought, effort and knowledge on a higher level of expression.

Transferring effort to higher goals, stimulated by humanitarian attitudes is the evolutionary step facing the race as it becomes polarized in the Aquarian Age. THE REAPER sheds light on the apparent injustices, upon the futility of selfishness, and upon the uninhibited radical trend. When the highest expression of the ideas embraced in Arcanum XIII becomes widespread, the rainbow of the Aquarian Age will flash in full color, lighting the way for the peoples of both worlds. Man will come of age in Aquarius.

Chapter XIV

Fluxing Of Polar Opposites

Words are used to convey meaning, yet each of us has had a different background so we associate different meanings with the same word or phrase. The two keywords used when reading Arcanum XIV, The Alchemist, have several meanings, all taking the same trend. This tarot card is read as regeneration or temperance. Regeneration means reestablished on a better basis, and the temperance is defined as habitual moderation in the indulgence of the appetites and passions.

To attain these attributes, a well formulated plan of action followed persistently is necessary. This calls for the Divine virtue of patience, well mapped by the zodiacal sign of Taurus. The advancement of self, and thus the soul, does not come about by leaps and bounds. Rather the results stem from steady persevering effort.

Arcanum XIV represents the fluxing of the polar opposites, or mental antidotes. Flux usually refers to the fusion of metals or minerals, as in the case where resin is applied to surfaces which are to be joined by soldering or welding in order to free them from oxide, thus promoting their union. When the minerals are more acid, or positive, just enough negative, or alkaline minerals need to be added to bring about balance. If the alkaline is predominant, then a balance is maintained by adding the right amount of acid.

When positive and negative, acid and alkaline, male and female, energies are of like volume and intensity, the component parts of each easily fuse and undergo a transmutation into a different and far more valuable product. A regeneration takes place. However, if either positive or negative elements are not balanced by the polar opposite, more energy than can be generated is needed to bring about the transmutation. Thus it is in handling the individual life.

We need to know with what we have to work. This is pictured clearly in the birth chart erected for a date, hour, and place of birth. We also need to know what to do about the trends found in that map. Applying the laws of occultism, which include astrology, psychology, alchemy, and the handling of imponderable forces, to our everyday life will assist in bringing about the individual transmutation.

Major Arcanum XIV is called the ALCHEMIST. In the illustration of this card the three letters at the bottom are (1-r) Nun (Hebrew), N (English) and Nain (Egyptian). At the top we find the corresponding number to be 14. The Roman numeral XIV designates the number of the Major Arcanum. The symbol of Taurus gives the astrological association.

Pouring the fluid of life back and forth from a golden urn to a silver one, the genie of the Sun wears a crown of flame showing that it is a spirit. Wings at the feet symbolize rapid movements. The free flow of fluid from one urn to the other signifies transmutation, the fluxing of positive and negative elements to bring about regeneration.

You may recall the interpretation of Arcanum VIII, where energies were pictured in the state of equilibrium. With that interpretation in mind, it is revealing to note that there are eight rays of the Sun showing behind the genie's hand. The ancient masons used this symbolism to portray that the positive, or masculine, forces of the universe are exactly balanced by the negative, or feminine forces. The genie has a cloak over his shoulder. The cloak signifies matter, and the genie, spirit. Here the meaning is conveyed that matter is perpetually impregnated by spirit.

Taken as a whole the picture tells of a chapter from the book of nature. The combination and interchange of masculine and feminine forces throughout nature work ceaselessly in all kingdoms of life to instigate and cause all movements and life. It forms a dramatic panorama of cosmic fluxing.

Transmutation of some sort is necessary to progress. Without it a state of stagnancy or retrogression results. The major policy of the universe is progress. Therefore each soul has its important work to do in the Great Evolutionary Plan.

Just as in any of our large industrial concerns today, universal progress is attained by specialization of parts, division of labor, and cooperation between functions. Each one of us is a workman in the cosmic organization. How we handle our inherited potentials will tell whether we are helping or hindering the whole.

A man is not hired unless there is a job for him to do. No soul is called into existence unless there is a part for it to play in the Great Plan. Thus the mere fact that we are here means there is a job for us to do. The kind of work for which the man is hired depends upon his ability. After he starts working in a well-managed organization he is given educational advantages which make possible advancement to a more responsible position.

So it is in the evolution of the soul. Where the man is trained by the industrial organization, the soul is trained by Nature to fulfill some one position for which he is best suited by temperament. It becomes obvious that both the organization and the individual soul would be at a disadvantage to train for something which would not express his inherent ability, struggling to fit a square peg into a round hole.

The Alchemist thus points to the use of practical occultism, and the sooner the better. By applying occult laws, we make a study of our own temperaments and abilities in order to learn what work we are best fitted for in the scheme of things. When our thoughts follow this trend, we are likely to have a warped vision. Our values are off center. More often than not we think that our cosmic mission is some earth-shaking action which will change our world over night.

But the truth of the matter is that each of us has certain potentials, aptitudes, and abilities which can be expressed in any department of life in a constructive manner at any time, thus adding something of value to the cosmic organization. A study of the individual birth chart will show what the potentials are. A study of the individual conditioning energy, resulting from how the person has thought, felt, and acted up to now, will reveal what he has done so far with the inherited potentials he brought with him to this life.

Prominent planets in a chart point out the potentials. Harmonious or discordant aspects of the planets will show the environment which will most likely be attracted and the obstacles he needs to overcome. As astrology is anything but fatalistic, with that information the person can go ahead to pattern his life, determining just how he is going to flux the mental energies he has within himself. He will know their specialized combinations through the aspects portrayed in his horoscope. By applying occult principles, he can transmute the discords to attract a better life.

Because of the widespread reaction toward the so-called discordant or afflicted aspects, I think it is important to stress that any aspect represents energy which must express. The square, semisquare, sesquisquare, and opposition aspects all map a discordant expression unless the energies they represent are transmuted. While the trine, sextile and semisextile are considered fortunate, they only express as "good" if the energies are released in a constructive channel.

From long experience in astrological research, it seems to me we should approach aspects in the chart like so: The discordant ones place friction and obstacles in the road, and the good ones map clear sailing. However, unless we capture and release the energies they map in a constructive way, both types can have an opposite reaction.

In my files there are several charts showing grand trines and all "good" aspects. None of these people ever really matured emotionally. Their case histories show little development of character. On the other hand, there is a chart where a trine (called the aspect of good luck) mapped a great loss into the life. However, even though the loss came, another action in the same department of life came as a blessing. There is much to be said along this line.

Have you ever noticed that many people who have contributed to our way of life, through the arts, science, professions, etc., have had severely afflicted horoscopes? Progress comes from surmounting obstacles. The extra effort expended develops the character thus fitting the native for bigger and better things. The "good" aspects are of the rocking chair type; one sits and rocks as time passes and no progress is made. The old rocker is comfortable, and until a different attitude is taken by stimulating desire to do, nothing results of any importance.

In deciding to live a better life, to regenerate, the greatest obstacle is taking the correct attitude. We often get so tied up with the business at hand that we forget the overall picture of just what we are trying to accomplish. In a general sense we are all fluxing our inherent mental elements, which are combined differently in each individual. If any soul is perfectly adjusted, there is no need for physical existence, which is nature's school for character education.

Each day is a cycle in itself. Whether yesterday was a bad day is of no consequence. The attitude of learning from the experiences is the important thing. Today we can try for success. It is a waste of the vital life force to spend it in regret. After all, no war is worn without losing some battles, nor will a new life pattern be established without experiencing days of defeat.

Victories and defeats occur each day. If we face that fact, less time will be spent in negative attitudes of disappointment, discouragement and regret. In occultism applied, corresponding to Arcanum XIV, one of the first things to learn is an attitude of constant vigilance toward the character of all thoughts, feelings and actions.

Each birth chart maps methods of transmuting discordant thoughts, feelings, and actions, but in general, anger should be converted into constructive activity. Irritability is childish; we are adult beings. Let's act, think, and feel the part. Nobody can irritate us unless we allow such a reaction.

As every bit of our vital energy must be used to carry out our plan of a patterned life, we cannot become devitalized by nourishing feelings of discouragement. In God's Great Plan, you always get another chance. The circumstances may be different, but the basic thread of experience is the same. At the very moment any of the emotions are stimulated, we can be on guard to redirect their energies. Just keeping the current boiling underneath will not do. All such feelings, whether expressed outwardly or not, are discordant and act as destructive forces.

A jangle of the nervous system expressing through electromagnetic energies carries the vibrations to the astral body where the discord is duplicated. It is how we think that attracts things into our lives, and the jangling astral thoughts attract inharmonious conditions. Understanding this law of nature reveals that one of the most unprofitable actions we can take is to harbor discordant feelings. The more discordant our thoughts, the more discord awaits us. We attract it through that type of thinking.

As the ensemble presented by Arcanum XIV points out, a well formulated plan of action persistently followed is necessary to regenerate the life. Fluxing the mental factors makes possible transmutation. Which factors need attention and how they should be handled is mapped by the symbology in the chart of birth.

Success of such a plan is not an instantaneous manifestation. The patience of Taurus is needed to acquire the proper habit systems that further four aims that result in happiness: 1)To find pleasure in all that one does, 2)To find work where one can give service to humanity, 3)To work to refine one's body, intellect, and feelings, and 4)To take the time to find harmonious channels for all of one's insistent desires.

Chapter XV

The Mark Of The Beast

Do you know the rewards of black magic? Are you a slave to psychological toll-gates? Do you know what false pride does to your soul? Is your life touched by the torch of destruction and misery? Do you know what the mark of the beast means?

Study and meditation on the fifteenth Major Arcanum of the sacred tarot, called the BLACK MAGICIAN, prompts questions and reveals answers that help to discern some of the workings of the Divine Plan.

In the illustrated Arcanum, the three letters at the bottom are (1-r) Samek (Hebrew), X (English) and Xiron (Egyptian). At the top we find the corresponding number to be 15. The Roman numeral XV designates the number of the Major Arcanum. The symbol of Saturn gives the astrological association.

Overshadowing the whole ensemble is Typhon, genius of evil, who takes a triumphant stand above the ruins of the fallen temple. Each bit of symbolism was used by the ancient masons to portray some spiritual concept of their philosophy. The scepter upon which rests a circle and two divergent bars, shown in Typhon's right hand, signify how inversive forces (spreading bars) hem in and hamper the influence of spirit (circle). In this way hatred and division was mapped. In his left hand Typhon holds the torch of destruction which he used to ruin the temple.

Emerging from his head is a flame, to indicate that he is not of this world. The fact that he is a denison from the realm of darkness is shown by the wings of a bat. Stubborn rebellion is indicated by the horn on his nose.

When expressed adversely, one of the most materialistic signs of the zodiac, the natural home of Saturn, is Capricorn, which is symbolized by the goat. The ancient masons placed goat feet upon Typhon and goat heads on the chained beings kneeling in the foreground to indicate that their in-

telligence was used for material and selfish ambitions. His head is that of a crocodile, representing cruelty.

The chained beings at the monster's feet picture the fate that comes to all who use magical powers to attain selfish or purely material ends. Eventually they are enslaved by the very forces they have used, and after passing to the next life are chained by their evil deed in the underworld. They are racketeers and gangsters on both planes. Taking the illustration as a whole, the concept presented indicates both the bondage and the fate of beings who follow the inversive path and become dominated by the spirit of selfishness.

In the Biblical story of the mark of the beast it tells how none shall buy or sell except those who have the mark of the beast in their hands and in their foreheads. Refer to Rev. 13:18: "Here is wisdom. Let him that hath understanding count the number of the beast . . . his number is six hundred three score and six." Note that number is not 666 as commonly quoted, but 600 three score and six. Adding the numbers, six plus three plus six equals 15. Through Arcanum XV the meaning of the mark of the beast becomes crystal clear, for it corresponds to Saturn, the safety urge, and the father of grasping selfishness.

The admonition associated with this Arcanum begins: "Remember then, son of earth, that the most unprofitable thing in the world is selfishness." Thinking of self to the exclusion of everything also does not prepare the soul to take up its habitation in the new life it finds after leaving the physical body.

Selfishness has a multitude of manifestations. It is combined with pride when it seeks to climb or advance by pulling someone else down. Selfishness is pure greed when using unfair advantage and methods to deprive another. Selfishness becomes black magic when using occult forces to take unfair advantage of another.

If we view each selfish thought as a Lilliputian person, view the subconscious mind, or soul, as a Gulliver, with each selfish thought having the ability to tie string upon the Gulliver of the soul, it is not so hard to realize that when enough small strings are tied to the soul, it becomes chained to earth, or earth-bound. There it may stay after transition as long as it remains self-centered.

Each unworthy thought adds energy of a discordant nature. By adding such energy it assists in lowering the basic character vibratory rate of the soul, thus creating a lower destiny for the person. When the soul leaves this physical earth it travels to a realm corresponding to its own basic vibratory rates. Further, it gravitates to a region in that realm or world, that most closely approximates all of the traits of character that have been built into the soul during its physical expression.

If selfish motives are used in pursuing this journey through physical life, the habitual attitude dominating the mirror of the mind revolves about the following thoughts: How can I get blank for me? How can I pull the other person down who stands in my way? How can I take advantage of my fellow man? How can I get glory of myself? How can I get the biggest house? If an attitude holds the greatest part of the attention regardless of the effect upon others, there is a successful building of a chain which holds the soul very close to physical earth when it leaves this life.

Taking this attitude insures that one must double pay for each step he advances. Because the energy has been expended in thinking evil and unworthy thoughts, an equal or greater amount of thought-energy has to be used in order to correct the errors in thinking and feeling that were indulged while still on earth.

By harboring unworthy thoughts, psychological toll-gates are erected upon the pathway of the soul, obstacles impossible to get around, to climb over or dodge through. Success means tearing down those same tollgates with the opposite type of thoughts and feelings than those with which they were built.

Every unworthy thought in the mind should be eradicated, and a worthy one put in its place. This supreme cost in effort shows that selfishness is the most unprofitable in the world.

If you want to move your residence it is not necessary to tear down the old house, dispose of the lumber and building materials, clean up the ground and make it appear as though a home had not been constructed there in the first place.

Yet, that is exactly when one has to do when he indulges in selfish and unworldly thoughts. The greater emotional association that is tied in with selfishness, the stronger the bars are erected across one's pathway to spiritual attainment, the greater the work that will have to be done to lower the bars clearing the pathway to soul advancement.

It is not always easy to cast out unworthy thoughts. The majority of human beings on earth are conditioned to think selfishly. The social structure in which we live views the acquisition of many material things as a distinct honor. If one collects enough material things for himself, it is not very hard to get accepted into what is called "good" society. It means that you can live in what are called "exclusive" neighborhoods, in a larger house than the other fellow's, and have a slew of servants to do your work for you. This state of affairs is usually viewed as a great achievement.

It certainly could be called that if one's needs were met and he had more time because of servants and the other things. Then he would be free to contribute his utmost to universal welfare.

On the other hand, the wish to gain all of these things may be the achievement of a soul who is very poor in spiritual things. So poor that when he leaves this little earth he will live in the astral hells. On that plane there is no light discernable to the eyes; no source of light, or a dim glow.

The denizens of this dark realm look like pirates were supposed to look, one eye gouged out and knife between the teeth. They travel with Typhon. These are the kind of faces you see, and that is the kind of place the individual who is considered eminently successful in the material world may well have built for himself. This could be attracted providing all of his moves were made for purely selfish reasons, with a great deal of emotion associated with looking out for number one.

But there is another type of person who makes no attempt to accumulate a lot of material things, cares little about worldly goods excepting only that the needs of the day are satisfied. He may devote a great deal of thought and effort to the problem of seeing what he can do about his own soul. In the environment he lives in, he tries to be a cooperative part of it, tries to help others, and learns to love his fellow man and all God's creatures through his observation and study of nature, sometimes with no formal education.

The difference in the richness these two people have laid up is astounding. The one, if he has no illusion about a great white throne, a ledger, a gavel, and a St. Peter sitting up there meting out justice, will gravitate to a relatively nice place, possibly around the third or fourth astral sphere. The other person, one who attains so much, who makes the news headlines, who is a great mind in the eyes of other selfish people, finds himself in the mires and morass of the astral hells, for that is the kind of character he has built.

Selfishness, while it may collect a vast amount of physical goods, builds the character of a beast. Although the first fellow's name never appeared in a newspaper and nobody ever heard of him on radio or television, he spent his life, in so far as he was able, in constructive endeavor. As a result his spiritual reward is certain.

A soul is attracted to the type of realm that corresponds exactly to its character. The law of affinity works. Like types of character are attracted to the types of realms, or like vibratory levels, which are worlds. The soul is attracted to the place in that realm which corresponds to all the personal quirks, which are now called personality complexes, where it will find other similar souls.

True intelligence demands that the individual use as much of his powers and possibilities as he possibly can, in order to adapt to the realities of life. These realities embrace not only the physical realm but expand beyond it into the astral, the spiritual and through life eternal.

By failing to consider adjustment to life as it really is, by spending all the time and energy trying to adjust to the illusion of life, one is enacting the role of Typhon, genius of evil.

"If Arcanum XV should appear in the prophetic signs of thy horoscope," said the ancient mason. "Cease to rely upon thine own power and wisdom and labor to disengage thyself from pride and selfishness, which but bind thee to matter, mortality and evil fate." Then you will avoid the Mark of the Beast.

Chapter XVI

Aggression In Spirituality

Mars, god of war, is most often associated in the minds of people with physical destruction, surgical operations, ammunition, and brute force. These things are intimately interpreted from the physical angle. Yet the two planes of ourselves include an inner life and an outer life. Another way of expressing the idea is the animal soul and the divine soul. Words are inadequate. Perhaps the psychological terminology of creative forces (building for the future) and destructive forces (death) would convey more meaning.

Regardless of the connotation put upon the several words, the universal truth shines through all as harmony is life, discord is death. Much good about this duality in man's nature can be gleaned from a study of the tarot. Every pictured lesson of the ancients brings out thoughts along this line. In Arcanum XVI, called THE LIGHTENING, more is revealed in universal language of the psychological principles involved.

There are some who think that exercising the Mars energies is an unspiritual act. But in the study of ancient masonry, we find that the lodge could not open until all were present. The soul cannot function on any plane without all of its parts. Mars is the astrological symbol corresponding to aggressiveness, a trait needed in all endeavors, physical, mental, and spiritual. Thus aside from the commonly accepted physical interpretation of Mars, there is a spiritual Mars which should be exercised if a healthy, strong spiritual body is to be built.

All of man's actions stem from the three hereditary drives. They are the drives for significance, for race preservation and for self preservation. Mars is the symbol for race preservation. All evolution in nature is pointed toward the development of these three drives.

Both race preservation and self preservation are selfish qualities, developed as the struggle for survival continued. Qualities directed to the destruction of enemies, and the gaining of food supply, regardless of the effect upon others, built self-centeredness. But in the act of preserving and providing for self and family, creatures built up initiative and an energy supply. This aggressiveness and energy is the force behind the animal soul of man, the human function to which Arcanum XVI corresponds.

Now we can begin to understand just what a spiritual Mars is. Man would have no force without animal energy. If he had no force, he would be unable to accomplish anything. The animal propensities are the only source of energy, and they form the bank from which man must draw to attain spiritual accomplishment. The force may express on the animal level if it is used for seeking selfish ends. The force may express on the spiritual level if it is used for seeking good for all. The latter is the expression of a spiritual Mars.

In the illustration at the bottom are (1-r) Ayi (Hebrew), O (English) and Olelath (Egyptian). At the top we find he corresponding number to be 16. The Roman numeral XVI designates the number of the Major Arcanum. The symbol of the planet Mars gives the astrological correspondence.

A great deal of action is shown by this card. There is nothing milk and water about it. Once the impetus is started, accident, or catastrophe results.

There are immutable laws in the universe, and they are not laid aside for any particular person or group. Taking up most of the illustration is a pyramid. The ancient wise men who designed the tarot cards used the pyramid, considered the most stable of solids, to symbolize the earth and to represent the peak of earthly security.

A strong correspondence exists between a birth chart and a pyramid. It is composed of four sides, each of which forms a trine. These correspond to the twelve (four times three) houses, or departments of life. Thus, it is a symbol of the horoscope of physical life.

Pictured atop the pyramid is a platform of seven stages, to represent the seven levels of physical development. Here man has reached the peak of earthly evolution. Just previous to the action portrayed here, two men are standing on that platform. You will note that one man wears a crown and the other does not. In this manner did the ancients signify that the universal laws, once set into motion, work regardless of who furnishes the trigger power. They say to us in symbolism: Nature is no respecter of persons, her laws operate the same for high born or low born, for kings or peons. She plays no favorites as she wields her universal justice.

A thunderbolt speeds through space, its flash lighting the ensemble, and it strikes the peak of the pyramid. The top is cut off, the platform falls, both the crowned and the uncrowned man tumble with the rest of the debris. The lesson which the sages meant to convey by this action is not as negative as it may sound. Rather, it lights the way to actions which will prevent such a downfall of any soul.

Further than that this ensemble symbolizes the false security that comes to those whose horizons end at purely physical and material success. It portrays the environment and actions attracted to oneself when magical forces are used to get selfish ends. It depicts enterprises that have not been thought out thoroughly as to the forces they may set into motion. It signifies ambitions and wishes which are frustrated, as well as projects which, because of the selfish or destructive action behind them, remain sterile.

The attitude of mind can prevent catastrophic results. That is an attitude which embraces intense motive, involving the thoughts, feelings, and actions, to assist in the greatest possible way the advancement of the universe, to enhance the happiness and usefulness of all life forms on earth. Eternal life is lived on an upward spiral, not horizontally.

Physiologists tell of the amazing machine this body of ours is. The functions are electrical in nature. But machines differ one from the other, each requiring a special skill to be handled efficiently. Knowledge and practice are needed to get the best results. Without knowledge and practice, it is impossible to fly an airplane. Without knowledge and practice it is impossible to operate a cyclotron. Man's body, being another kind of machine, also requires knowledge and practice if it is expected to run efficiently.

The body is the vehicle of the soul, and without the soul, the body would disintegrate to pass from the realm of physical manifestation. The most potent power to run this physical machine is the mind. Thus every thought, feeling, and action determines what the results will be.

In his book *The New Model of the Universe*, Ouspensky says: "An idea is a machine of enormous power." He refers to an idea as a complicated machine, which to be handled requires a lot of theoretical knowledge, experience, and practical training. The psychological ideas the ancient magi depicted are well summed up in his statement: "Unskilled handling of an idea may produce an explosion of the idea; a fire begins, the idea burns, and consumes everything round it."

An idea is like everything in the universe; it does not stand alone. If an idea "explodes," a chain reaction of the same nature can run a disastrous course as it sucks in other ideas. If this occurs, soon the dominant vibration is lowered to the point where catastrophe will end the chain reaction.

Magic and its fundamentals are also part of the universal concept conveyed by Arcanum XVI. One principle illustrated, in the words of C.C. Zain. "Any destructive force sent against another, when the period of its orbit has been completed, will return to inflict punishment upon the sender." In other words, if the climb in attaining the peak of physical security, disregarding the spiritual phases of life, is brought about with force and selfishness, by pulling others down in order to raise self; then punishment results.

The very act of sending a destructive image or thought to another demands that first it be formed in the astral body of the sender. As this astral body is fed, formed, and molded by the thoughts we think, destructive thoughts become the seat for an astral cancer. As soon as the orbit of the idea is completed, the energy put behind it returns home to encourage the malignant thought-cells to do the business they were designed to do.

A nucleus of evil itself attracts influences of like nature to vitalize the colony of sells eating into the healthy tissue of the astral form. When the work is done, and it can be done very efficiently if the sender of such thoughts makes a practice of this principle, the very force which was at first directed out to another brings misfortune.

Let's shift to the other side of the fence for a moment. What about the receiver of such black thoughts? He has a role in this astral orgy. Does he know how to play it? The best way to increase any invisible evil astral force is to fight it. In order to fight a thing, you have to give it your attention. Thus the act of fighting the invisible force keeps one tuned in on its low vibratory rate. There are ways the receiver of an evil thought can play his role to protect himself from a black blast.

He can build a protection of cold reflective armor about himself which will effectively hold out the vibrations. However, in so doing he may also render himself unreceptive to the beneficent influences flashed his way. The second method is the safest of all and most effective.

To understand this method of protection, a natural law must be considered. Nothing can reach our consciousness unless we tune in on its level. The safe method of protecting oneself from evil thoughts projected by another is to tune in on something entirely different, something on which pleasure and intensity can be brought to bear. It is only when the attention is completely captured that the lower vibrations of the evil thought cannot penetrate.

Thus we see the principle of magic working from both sides of the fence, evil thoughts in their relation to the sender and the receiver. Mental magic is a weapon used by the dark forces.

Mental magic is not a necessary tool in the spiritual climb to the top of the pyramid, from which the spiritual Mars operates to carry the soul on to greater heights. It is the transmuting of the animal soul into the divine soul as symbolized by Arcanum XVI.

Chapter XVII

Kinship Of All Life

"Remember, then, son of earth, that hope is the sister of faith. Shed thy passions and thy errors in order to study the mysteries of true science and the key will be given thee; then a ray of divine light will break from the occult sanctuary in order to dissipate the shadows of thy future and show thee the way of happiness." - C.C.Zain

One of the most intriguing patterns for investigation is the law of association in its relation to what we think. Perhaps you can remember a stimulating conversation with a friend, where the subject matter possibly started with the weather, then hopped to astrology and eventually wound up in an inspiring give and take on philosophy. After such a stimulating exchange, it is most interesting to go back and unweave the pattern by association. One thing reminds us of another, and it, in turn, brings to mind something entirely different. Soon the fabric of association leads us far afield of the original topic.

In gathering papers in preparation for this book, something of the sort happened to me. Before writing each chapter on the tarot, I usually read the admonition, because it seems to attune me to the spiritual and psychological side of the subject more effectively than anything else. It is truly wonderful how the ancient magi presented the universal truths in this fashion. However, if anything is to have meaning for me as an individual, I need to associate it with something in my present environment.

When I read the admonition of Arcanum XVII taken from *The Sacred Tarot*, my thoughts gathered and concentrated on one phrase: "Shed thy passions and thy errors in order to study the mysteries. . ." These words seem to be printed in neon lights. Why, I asked myself, should these particular words impress me so strongly?

Commonly we all ask ourselves questions. Consensus of opinion is that if you do not answer out loud you can escape the white-coated men!

But in all seriousness each of us has his own approach. With me, it has to be personal to please my Aries Sun sign. All experiences and memories are stored in the subconscious mind. It is there that we find the answers and associations. I have nicknamed my subconscious mind "Butch."

After reading that neon-lighted phrase again, I settled back in my chair and told Butch to go to work on the question. Sometimes the rascal will not follow such an order. After all, the subconscious is ruled by the changeable Moon. However, I had asked the question on one of his good days.

He gave me a string of impressions: A phone call from one of my students; a lecture I had attended at the Manuscripters Club;

and a book I had recently read which furnished me with one of the most delightful experiences I had had in a long time. These formed the threads in the pattern. Lazily, Butch and I unraveled the pattern.

That day when I answered the phone, the excited voice of my student told me about a wonderful book. She urged me not to miss it. In fact, she was so impressed that she had phoned the author and was most enthusiastic that I contact him to speak at one of our Starlight dinners held each month. Busy! Busy! Busy! That described my life for the next couple of months. So I had not looked into the book.

Then I decided I needed to get some Venus (social activity) to balance so much responsibility (Saturn). Again, I attended a Manuscripters meeting. That night the speaker was J. Allen Boone, author of *Kinship With All Life*. Book and author were the same which had so enthused my student. I was stimulated beyond words, for here was a man speaking about things just a decade ago would have branded him "a bit off." I bowed to Butch for having impressed me to go to that meeting.

In his humorous, easy and flowing style, Mr Boone writes along the same vein as that expressed in the phrase from the admonition. He is a former newspaper man who has traveled the length and breadth of the earth, lived in the jungles, rubbed shoulders with the masses in India, interviewed political diplomats and pioneered in Hollywood films.

But the one experience in his long colorful career which he claims revolutionized his life was the realization of a cosmic "something" that he tells about in his fascinating book. In it, he realizes how he had to shed his prejudices and preconceived ideas to become humble. He stresses that unless humility is present, communication with all life is not readily gained.

Using animals in his experiments, he has told in a most engaging fashion just how to utilize some of the basic universal truths passed on to us down through the ages. If you have a pet, you will understand him better after reading this book in which "intelligent" humans and "dumb" animals are revealed in the light of the cosmic "something."

Apropos to the subject is a passage starting on page 331 of *The Sacred Tarot*. If in those pages you read about communications between humans and their pets who have passed to the next plane of existence, more meaning of the kinship with all life will impress you. Here again association enters to bring a fuller meaning about just what the "kinship" is that exists between all life.

Perhaps you are wondering what all this has to do with the tarot. Mercury is pictured with wings on his feet to symbolize speed and alertness. The qualities of the dual sign Gemini, which is ruled by Mercury, follow the same pattern. As with everything else that comes under the scrutiny of an astrological student's eye, the symbolism of the corresponding tarot card will shed deeper insight and open vistas unthought of before. The book of nature can be open by two keys only: The silver key that corresponds to the tarot and the golden key corresponding to astrology. Blending of two forms is the triangle of knowledge and realization.

Major Arcanum XVII is called THE STAR. The three letters at the bottom of the illustration are (1-r) Pe (Hebrew), F-P-PH (English) and Pilon (Egyptian). At the top we find the corresponding number to be 17. The Roman numeral XVII designates the number of the Major Arcanum of the Egyptian. The astrological correspondence of the card is the zodiacal sign Gemini.

Eye catching are two factors: The nude maiden and the star over her head. Her state of nudity represents a universal reality. In order to see and understand truth, one must be stripped of dogmatic opinions, preconceived ideas and prejudices, which are nothing but the garments fashioned from the artificialities of civilization.

The cups she holds in her hands are made of the same materials as the two keys which unlock the cycles of nature, gold and silver.

She rests partly on land and partly on sea, to signify that truth is dual, the truth of reality and the truth of appearances. From the silver cup is her right hand, she pours a fluid into the sea, denoting that the loving and emotional side of man's nature must be nourished so that he may grasp the inner truth. Silver refers to the all-inclusive philosophy of the sacred tarot.

In the other hand she pours fluid from a golden cup onto the earth, to indicate that if man is to progress he needs to cultivate the positive, reasoning intellect within his nature. Gold refers to astrology, a study of which brings to man just those individual experiences he needs and how to meet and handle the events that come into his life. Then he can possess outer truth.

Nourishment provided both on the inner plane and on the outer plane, if carefully selected and assimilated, assists in attaining the revelation of the truth of realities.

Duality is again symbolized in the brilliant star of eight rays containing two trines. Here is symbolized the Law of Equilibrium, the balance between spirit and matter, male and female, inner and outer. The two trines, black symbolizing material and white the spiritual also portray the dual interpretation.

The fluid the girl pours from the golden cup represents the forces of man, while the fluid of the silver cup represents the forces of woman. Here we have the blending of positive and negative forces whose finer energies bring transmutation and combine to form the fluid of universal life.

Surrounded by seven smaller stars or seals, the large star represents the book of the apocalypse sealed with the seven seals. Occult interpretation of this symbolism shows the inner realization and the outer realization, the birth of the soul and the birth of the body, both influenced by the so-called basic seven planets.

Portraying the Hermetic Axiom "As above, so below" are two trines representing the universal truth that experiences, both good and evil, are necessary for soul progression. If the soul assimilates its experiences it is assured of immortality as symbolized by the butterfly perched on three blossoms (three planes of existence) where it sips the nectar of wisdom.

Gemini is the most dual sign of the zodiac. Appropriately it is pictured by the constellation of the twins. Reason and intuition are its tools. When wielded with skill these tools sustain all worlds and make life and consciousness possible.

To tap the elixir of spiritual life, prejudices and preconceived ideas must be cast aside and the immortal fountain at the Divine Source approached with humility. Keyword of the card: Truth, Hope or Faith.

It is in these attributes that the neophyte contacts Mr. Boone's "cosmic something." It is the way of knowing the kinship of all life which is written in the book of nature and unlocked by the two keys. The Star of Truth lights the way.

Chapter XVIII

Controlling Occult Forces

Cancer, ruled by the Moon, is the astrological correspondence to Major Arcanum XVIII in the sacred tarot. More than any other sign of the zodiac, Cancer is susceptible to influences from the environment, both physical and non-physical. Everything, including people and objects, radiates a certain signatory vibration to which Cancer tends to react pronouncedly. It easily picks up and interprets thoughts of entities living in non-physical worlds. This Arcanum, therefore, is naturally associated with the occult science of mediumship.

Everything in the universe is to a degree mediumistic; where the passive always becomes the medium of the active, an immutable law of nature. A medium is something that receives and transmits force. For example, matter is the medium for the expression of mind. Passive things are those which are acted upon, while active things are those which exert energy to produce change in the passive.

How is it determined which is active and which passive? At first, one might jump to the conclusion that the thing with the greatest volume of energy was the active. However, this is not necessarily the truth of the matter. The volume of energy is not the determining factor. Rather the relative activity of whatever energy is present will tell if the thing under consideration is active or passive.

Energy is transformed in a million different ways. Energy is never lost, a transfer always takes place, nature's conservation of energy. Thus everything is in motion, even those things that appear stationary to our dull perceptions. Motion implies that something is acting as a medium for the transmission of energy. Look at man! He is different from all other living things, because he has learned how to use and control a great number of complex forces in his functioning.

Astrology is the golden key that unlocks the mysteries of nature. It is the most perfect instrument by which to interpret man's true relation to the universe. A tool only, astrology is the yardstick for measuring the energies and forces that are captured, stored, and released by man. Because the energies of the interior planes are more active than those external, the physical becomes the medium to the astral. It is in this manner that astrological forces influence life in the material world.

Life is being influenced by unseen currents of energy radiated by the planets every single moment. A magnetic sympathy pervades all nature, thus similar qualities are expressed in octaves. The planetary affinity of an object is designated by planetary rulership.

By going to a higher octave, we are justified in saying that the astral world must be passive to energies being radiated from the spiritual world. To complete the picture, we climb the octaves of nature and say that God is the central controlling force of the universe. Our octaves of energy expression then range from Him down to the densest mineral atom, showing a complete graded scale of mediumship, each higher plan transmitting the One Universal Force to the plane next below, until finally it reaches and energizes the lowest level.

Those called masters or adepts are mediums for the transmission of spiritual ideas to the physical plane. They are taught on interior planes and externalize what they receive. For this reason a true adept never claims to originate the teachings he gives out. He has received them from exalted beings who have in turn received the information from still more interior worlds. The links continue to the very throne of God, the absolute source of truth.

However, there is a great difference between the conscious and controllable mediumship as just explained and the disintegrative type where a person trusts a discarnate entity to control and use his body as a means of communication. Again, this emphasizes the fact that just because something comes from an interior plane, it is not necessarily constructive. The neophyte is warned about these forces in symbolical language, as we see in the interpretation of Arcanum XVIII.

How can we explain the relationship of astrological energies and their tie-up with the units in the universe? Man's astral body, as well as the astral counterparts of things, contain energy centers which are keyed to each of the planets. But in one person or thing an energy center keyed to one planet may be as weak that no response is felt. On the other hand, another energy center keyed to a different planet may be so strong and active as to overshadow other influences.

Due to the law of sympathetic vibratory response all persons and things transmit the influence of every planet to some degree.

More often than not, the energy center transmitting the astral vibrations of some one planet is more prominent than the other centers. When its key is determined, the person or thing is said to be ruled by that planet because it is the strongest and most active influence in the makeup.

A chain of mediumship takes place when astrological energies impinge upon the subconscious mind of man. The subconscious mind becomes the medium for the transmission of energy. Energy stimulates thoughts and feelings which produce motion in environment. Environment reacts to produce what is usually called event. Thus a chain of actions and reactions, constituting a form of mediumship, is set into motion.

It is through astral vibrations that each planet sends a special grade of energy; its motivation is determined by the sign of the zodiac; its direction by the horoscope house; and its constructive or destructive potential is mapped by astrological aspects but subject to control by directed thinking.

Moods is the keyword of Cancer. A dominant mood determines the level of things contracted, and life forms have the peculiar power of absorbing and transmitting the energies of the surrounding atmosphere. If the elixir of life is pure, absorption, and transmission of only the finer and higher life-giving energies take place. Yet, if impure, grosser energies are attracted, Arcanum XVIII may represent either one. Therefore, it is understandable that the keywords associated with this tarot card are: deception, false friends, or secret foes.

Let us look at the tarot symbolism. Major Arcanum XVIII is called THE MOON. The three letters at the bottom of the illustration (1-r) are Tzaddi (Hebrew), SH-TS-TZ (English) and Tsaidi (Egyptian). At the top, we find the corresponding number to be 18. The Roman numeral XVIII designates the number of the Major Arcanum of the Egyptian tarot. The astrological correspondence of the card is the zodiacal sign of Cancer.

The silvery Moon rides through a night sky studded with nebulous gray clouds. A neophyte stumbling along the pathway of eternal progression, in a moment of impatience at his progress, lowers his spiritual standards. By thinking negatively he becomes moody and susceptible to the environment. If his guard stays down as he enters new occult fields, he will invite deception and will falsely interpret the objects in his pathway.

This dim moonlight scene could portray the seance room, where hidden perils abound, yet are covered with the silvery glamour of the pale moonbeams. For here all types of influences gather, a conglomerate vibration which bombards the neophyte, who needs be on his guard against invasion.

Because he is negative at the time, wanting a word of encouragement from the beyond, he does not realize that here are congregated the good, the bad, the ignorant, the learned. Attracted to the scene are lying spirits, friendly spirits, treacherous spirits, dominating spirits.

The pictured objects stand at the edge of the road leading to the "beyond," the "soul world" or the "mansion of life after death." Each object symbolizes the varied influence there. The two pyramids represent life. The black one indicating the 12 houses of the horoscope denotes an ignorant and unspiritual life, while the white one symbolizes a learned life enlightened by science and a spiritual wisdom. Note the door, or exit, in the white pyramid signifying the enlightened spiritual people are not earth-bound, but after physical death pass freely to a life in the higher spheres.

In the road immediately in front of the pyramids are three objects. The black dog shows the presence of lying spirits whose hostile minds will surround the neophyte with ambushes. The white dog shows friendly spirits whose servile minds will offer the neophyte flatteries. The scorpion crawling in a circle of white denotes treacherous minds who plan to get their selfish ends through the neophyte's own ruin. The white circle represents the knowledge they put to selfish use in dominating and controlling the neophyte.

Before he crosses the boundary to the soul world, whether for a visit or to make permanent residence, the neophyte should study the neighborhood he wishes to contact in that world. The soul world closest to the earth is the lower astral, where he will meet earth-bound souls (with fanatic fixations), vicious elementals, depraved elementaries, and a host of other entities. Some of these entities are harmlessly mischievous, some are inimical to the neophyte, and some desire to consume him for their own ends.

Should the neophyte choose this neighborhood, he will abdicate rulership of his body and attract domination by the entities who will use their advantage to deceive, demoralize, and obsess him. His will will be broken.

Masters tell us that knowledge or spirituality is not acquired by the mere transition from the earth plane to the astral. Consciousness of the neophyte remains at the same level which it was on earth until he makes progress through his own efforts.

After the neophyte has successfully passed the initiation pictured by Arcanum XVIII in his soul's pilgrimage, his mission in the astral world is to help free earth-bound souls from their fetters, to assist those souls deceived by lower entities to realize their powers, and to encourage them to strive for a new and better life.

Everything in the universe is in motion, acting as mediums for the absorption and transmission of energy. Arcanum XVIII points to the octave expression in the links of the mediumistic chain. He says, "Observe, listen! Do not deceive yourself, not drink of false elixir and become drugged into a semiconscious state in which you are unable to perceive the approach of your own downfall."

To understand the universe, it is necessary to explore secret realms. Such experience is not without perils. The only shining armor which will guard the neophyte exploring alone is a marked spiritual development whereby he has built himself a vigorous spiritual body. The other positive way to explore the secret realms is at the hand of a competent master who has learned to control occult forces.

Chapter XIX

Love And Soul Development

Leo, governing the heart and the sympathies, denotes the kind of love that springs unselfishly into existence, as the result of natural harmony. In the horoscope, Leo has natural rulership over the fifth house, or department of life, associated with pleasure, joy, happiness, children, and love affairs among other things. When the energies represented are channeled properly, the soul ascends to a golden spiritual throne, where it wields the spiritual light with its wide knowledge of universal law.

Arcanum XIX was used by the ancient magi to represent that imponderable force so valuable to man called inspiration, an indrawing of the spirit. The true source of all life, energy, and spiritual power is the Sun, whose home sign is Leo, the heart center of man through which the Sun pours its greatest volume of inspirational power. Thus we can say that Leo indicates the capacity to receive inspiration. Love, ruled by Leo, is acknowledged in most religions and philosophies to be the force that opens inspirational gates.

In the illustration, the three letters at the bottom are (l-r) Quoph (Hebrew), Q (English) and Quitolath (Egyptian). At the top we find the corresponding number to be 19. The Roman numeral XIX designates the number of the Major Arcanum of the sacred tarot. The symbol of the zodiacal sign Leo signifies the astrological correspondence.

Inspiration is the human function portrayed by the huge Sun overshadowing the lovers who stand holding hands within a circle of twenty flowers. The Sun symbolizes perfect union being expressed on three planes or levels. These are the perfect harmony of physical desires, intellectual interest, and spiritual aspirations. The 20 flowers springing from the earth denote the potential of domestic harmony to awaken and resurrect (keywords of Arcanum XX) the spiritual flora of the soul.

This symbolism shows the joy and happiness of the domestic circle which overshadows the material hardships and adjustments they must endure to reach this sublime state. In the center of the Sun is the symbol of conjugal union. The 21 rays emanating from the Sun denote success and attainment (keys of Major Arcanum XXI).

Plainly dressed by the ancient magi, the lovers stand for simplicity of life, moderation of desires and purity of thought. When the sexes are truly wed and obey the triple laws of harmony, their lives are filled with joy and happiness even when material loss and obstacles occur. The ensemble personifies the union of souls harmonious on all planes: For spiritual advancement, for producing and rearing children, and for the joyous experience of a home.

Such potent and harmonious vibrations are set into motion so that the sacrifices necessary to maintain a home and rear children are welcomed. These are important factors in soul development.

Ancient alchemists associated this Arcanum XIX with the drinking of the true elixir of life. However, it was not considered a matter of approaching the spiritual counter to order a cup and gulping the contents to walk out completely changed. Spiritual growth and the understanding of self-conscious immortality, the divine mission of the soul, is the result of the gradual changes set up in the finer forms by the elixir.

C.C. Zain writes of this concept poetically: "This Elixir is really a love potion, and the result of quaffing it is a general and complete harmonizing of all the internal vibratory rates, so that they sound a sweet and powerful chord, the pitch of which gradually rises as the body and desires are refined, and in time thus results in youthful vigor added to perpetual life."

Let us think of this concept for a moment in physical terms only. Perhaps we have all witnessed the change in middle-aged people who have fallen in love. The Elixir goes to work, and they both appear younger, act younger, and talk younger. Not that we should make a fetish of youth, which in my opinion we are inclined to do, but rather let us focus our attention on the mental outlook which is usually associated with youth.

Enthusiasm, which vitalizes current thoughts, stirs both the mind and the environment in a way that nothing else can. This vital mind aspect is the priceless part of the "youth" concept. The experiments of psychologists and philosophers have borne this out.

Now let us raise our sights to the inner planes where substances have an almost instantaneous response to the type of thought and feeling fed them. A mood of exalted love can feed the inner man food of good spiritual nourishment. After assimilation, these vibrations of a higher order penetrate all three planes, and the composite form is one of a highly refined nature.

Because the type of dominant vibratory rate we habitually hold determines the type of environment, both inner and outer, we attract to ourselves, it goes without saying that in cultivating a highly refined vibration we likewise attract the highly and refined environments. Then we have, figuratively, a good deposit in the spiritual bank.

True, we start with physical love, but that is only the beginning. As the soul develops, and it is so when two souls are working out their development together, the desires and attentions swing in an ever-widening circle. The direction is from self, to mate, to offspring and then on to everything in God's universe.

This process does not show a sharp shift of the love from one thing to another. Rather, there is a growth just as the physical example of a full course dinner implies. Each course is consumed, and if the diet is balanced, provides the necessary elements, and the food tastefully prepared and served, the blending of the total intake results in a good feeling of ease and comfort. So it is with the expanding love principle.

Just because we love our children when they come along, it does not follow that we love our mate any the less. Nor does it follow that when the children leave home to make a life of their own and we turn our love outward to include the wider concepts of life that we love our children less. Instead, our capacity and depth to love increases with each new experience and raises the love we have already developed to new heights.

"Universal love" is an abstraction which is difficult to understand when we first hear of it. But if we start with one thing, if no person is available, there are birds, trees, flowers, and other children of nature that respond to love, and learn to love that one thing unselfishly and unpossessively, then we can expand to include the other phases of the universe. Because we are placed here on the physical school of nature, it is necessary that we start small at the bottom of the evolutionary ladder then branch out our love to include the larger concepts.

If Mrs. Jones who lives down the street makes your skin crawl, it will be impossible to love all of God's plan. Highly evolved teachers tell us that there is only one prescription for this particular ailment. Look for the good things in Mrs. Jones, the God-like parts which are truly there and could be encouraged with vital attention.

If such an approach is demonstrated, then the kindly, impersonal feeling, but a confident feeling with faith at its shoulders, walks with you through the byways of life. Universal love becomes a glowing beacon lighting the spiritual pathway of the soul.

Spiritual progress depends upon love, unselfishness, and the refinement of the thoughts and emotions. Spiritual progress demands that the soul adjust to the physical environment. Some minds associate spirituality with do-nothingness, with avoiding all discord, with complete indrawing. If these are practiced, can we say that the neophyte is truly contributing to the divine plan?

Practicality is needed to develop spirituality, because the only method mother nature has of educating us is to encourage us to overcome obstacles. By doing so we develop our spiritual muscles.

Yet, I have encountered people over the years who talk of spirituality and the only impression given is that one should sit up there on a fluffy pink cloud, dangling rosy toes in order to keep out of "those low vibrations."

Well, God created it all, and all of it, no matter how horrible or distasteful some of it may seem, is there for a reason. The ancient magi have tried to portray the needed lesson for the neophyte, who, when he applies the lesson, experiences Joy and Happiness.

Arcanum XIX symbolizes the lesson on how to develop that precious human function called inspiration. Organic alchemy is the occult science associated with this tarot card. This Arcanum signifies a deep drive to become a valuable cell in the universal organism by the application of love on all levels to insure the neophyte's soul development.

Chapter XX

Immortality Of The Soul

Have you given serious thought to physical death? Paradoxical as it may sound, death is an important factor in eternal life. There are all sorts of deaths. Some occur every single second of the day and night. It is amazing how many people are afraid to die. Some years ago when the first atomic bombs shadowed the land, we received a great many letters in which fear of death was expressed in just as many ways.

In one sense, it is understandable that such a reaction should prevail. Most people are materialists, believing that their lives are completely expressed on one plane only, the physical.

The initiate knows that man is a two-plane organism. He knows man's life is not confined to physical nourishment and expression alone. Until the neophyte understands the inter-penetration of the two planes, he knows no better than to be afraid to die.

The ancient magi told of death and its purpose when they drew the symbolism for Major Arcanum XX, called the SARCOPHAGUS. If that word appears strange, consult a dictionary. The first meaning given: A limestone used among the Greeks for coffins, because it disintegrated their contents within a few weeks. Another definition given: A stone coffin.

Dominating the pictured symbolism in the illustration is the coffin. However, the other objects gain meaning in relation to it. The three letters at the bottom of the illustration are (1-r) Resh

(Hebrew), R (English), and Rasith (Egyptian). In using the Hermetic system of names and numbers (see Table II), this information means that the letter R is associated with the Moon. When you understand the astrological significance of the Moon, you then apply these factors to the subject you are considering numerologically.

At the top of the illustration we find the number 20. The Roman numeral XX designates the number of the Major Arcanum of the Egyptian tarot. The astrological correspondence of the card is the luminary Moon.

When reading this card in a tarot spread, the key is Awakening or Resurrection. We have heard these words so often that we have a tendency to skim over the meaningful depths implied. However, the Moon rulership gives a clue to interpretation. Everything in the universe, even that which seems most stable, is changeable. The impressionable nature of the Moon ties in with the factor of change. Without change there is no opportunity for development or evolution.

Thus change, the most important thing in the world, is at the base of all growth just as the tides correspond to the phases of the Moon are behind the element which assist in physical growth.

Notice the scarab on the side of the coffin. It is placed there for a reason: To symbolize the immortality of the soul. Changes come, environments shift, viewpoints alter, but the soul is never lost as it travels the spiral of eternal life. It is immortal, and physical death cannot change its destiny.

The call to the higher spheres is represented by a genie blowing a trumpet. At this call, the coffin opens and a man, woman, and child rise from within, still dressed in their winding sheets. Note that they rise in unison. The magi pictured them that way to indicate that immortality depends upon the trinity of positive and negative soul-monads united about their Deific Ego (the spark behind the soul). They drew a child to represent the ego, because it is innocent. The sarcophagus is the tomb through which the soul is promoted to a higher life in nature's evolutionary plan.

A limestone coffin is symbolical, because the real tomb is the physical body that confines and envelops the soul while it is developing its potentials through the functions of social life. This involves the soul's relations not only to people but to other life-forms as well.

Life is one; it is of a unity; and the apparent body which envelops it at anytime is always temporary. After experiencing life in one human form, the soul has acquired self-consciousness and does not need to return to earth. A resurrection and awakening to the new life takes place.

Another symbol is the trinity rising from the tomb together. The ancient masons used this to indicate that there are just as many opportunities for family life and other experiences on the next plane of life. The complete ensemble shows this entering into a new and active life in a realm above matter; the raised lid indicates the soul's flight out of matter and out of the physical body.

If I should tell you that I was going to take a trip from Sacramento to Paris next week, you would probably wish me well and hope I would have a good time. But if I told you that I was going to die next week, you would probably feel shock, horror, or any similar emotions. However, dying is really no different from moving out of one locality into another. Your neighborhood is not too different, especially at first, because you gravitate immediately after death to the corresponding level which matches your dominant vibratory rate.

Of course, what you do in the way of development after reaching your new location is, as it is here on earth, entirely up to you. On both planes there are those people whose lives are dedicated to disseminating knowledge which will assist you to make the transition gracefully and to progress in the building of your spiritual body. They do not seek you. You must of your own sincere desire want to improve. When this desire becomes strong and you vitalize it sufficiently, the teacher will appear.

Sometimes when we are thinking of occult things, we are inclined to drape our mental pictures with pink chiffon and purple velvet. But to come right down to this plane here and now, here is an example of what I really mean by "wanting to know."

As a youngster I knew nothing about astrology or occultism. Then a drastic event in my life forced me to ask, "What is life all about?" At the time I spent almost five days on the inner plane. It was only the persistence of my mother, appealing to my strong sense of smell with the earthy marigold, that brought me back. After passing through this period, I started asking for my cosmic work. I prayed fervently and tried to live in such a manner that it would be revealed to me. Experiences I had were out of this world and I mean that literally.

It took eight years to get the answer, which, by the way, was right under my nose all of the time. Being young, I had not had the experience necessary to develop the consciousness to understand these things. When the awaking came, it was like Arcanum XX, resurrection. There have been other awakenings since, there will be more links of change for progress.

Unless you have had some such experience or have made the contact with the inner planes directly, you may have a tendency to fear death. This is a negative state and something should be done about it. I would suggest to a person who harbors this fear (mental poisoning) to investigate the subject. A splendid reference on such matters, presented in a positive, understandable manner, is the book entitled *The Next Life*.

When anything is a mystery, it is easy to develop fear or reverence about it. But when the mysterious folds are peeled away with factual understanding, fear is dispelled. Death and the after-life have been discussed by many, many writers and philosophers who have experienced life there. Most of them bring back the same reports.

My favorite is the book mentioned above. My first reading impressed me with some of the things I had already discovered. But after really getting into it, my contacts become stronger and new vistas opened before me. A truly wonderful experience!

Did you know that pleasure is most important on the next plane? Of course we will still have our personal problems. Thank God! Would it not be boring to pluck harp strings and preen feathers 24 hours a day? That book tells of three methods of entering and exploring the next plane, what happens when you get there, what you can expect life to be while there, and how long you will visit that neighborhood.

As the twentieth century comes to an end, the planetary positions signal us that there will be many opportunities to develop character by using the principle of change in overcoming obstacles.

Everyone is being forced to adjust to changes, but in facing these vacillating conditions a heavy net of insecurity could entangle those who do not build up the positive nature within themselves. Sometimes that sort of insecurity turns to thoughts of death.

Should you experience such fear, do something about building up your faith. Faith without works is dead. That Biblical phrase warns to learn all you can and take constructive action, having faith that all will turn out according to the Divine Plan and Purpose.

When such an attitude is built into the character, then dying will seem like moving from one city to another. There is nothing to fear. One universal truth is the immortality of the soul.

Chapter XXI

Spiritual Pathway To Adeptship

One of the most remarkable wonders of our universe is the unfolding potentials of a soul as it develops from the first stumbling steps of the neophyte through various grades of manifestation to the positive exercising of the functions of adeptship. But a more wonderful spiritual principle insuring security is that no soul is ever lost, and all souls are offered an opportunity to travel the spiritual pathway under immutable laws operating within the Divine Plan.

On the physical plane the grand climax of evolution is the attainment of adeptship. Seven is the physical number. Although it is not easy to identify them, there are seven grades of humanity living on earth. The seventh, or highest, is the state of man.

Many pathways lead to the goal, adeptship. Under universal law each soul has the free will to select his own route within the framework of his individual divine destiny. Brought into being to fulfill a cosmic mission, the soul is confined to the development of certain potentials which will enable it to do its work. However, this does not deny free will choice.

True, each soul needs certain experiences. But there is a choice as to the manner in which it gains development through these experiences. To understand divine justice, we have to recognize that no two souls need the same experience, nor does any soul need all experiences. Divine order demands the conservation of energy. As the soul occupies the physical body of man only once, it attracts exact experiences it needs to gain its particular education while on the physical plane. Selection of a particular route to the goal is determined by behavior patterns, the grade of thoughts, feelings, and actions.

Despite the varied pathways, there is a broad, general pattern laid out for the neophyte to follow. To gain adeptship, the earnest neophyte engages a system of study in order to master the various branches of occult science. He undertakes a routine of regular psychic training. When he learns to use his inner faculties with accuracy, he has mastered the 21 lucidic arts. During this regime he works to develop seven states of consciousness, making up soul attainment. Adding the numbers: 21 plus 21 plus seven equals 49.

The same result is obtained by adding crosswise the factors in the word adept: A (1), D (4), E (5), P (17), T (22), equals 49, which is seven times seven. The perfect man, or adept, must be master of three times seven Sacred Sciences, three times seven Lucidic Arts and seven states of Soul Consciousness.

The man, or word, or number, is itself one, which added to the 49 totals 50, the number of Jubilee. This symbolizes the conscious transition of the physical Adept to become a Hierophant on the spiritual plane. 50 relates to soul mates, or the completion of the soul's cycle of necessity through involution and evolution.

There can be no permanent union of soul mates until each soul develops its spiritual faculties to a high order. As spiritual bodies are not inherited, part of each soul's mission is to build a vigorous spiritual body by living the life of the spirit. Strong magnetic attractions between the sexes, always revealed by a comparison of natal horoscopes, is often misunderstood as the meeting of soul mates.

Because cognition of soul mates is impossible until both souls have developed finer forms, the search for its mate while the soul is still functioning in a physical body is premature. When both souls have developed adeptship, recognition of the soul mate comes without effort. Because the joining of soul mates is regulated by immutable law, as is all else in the universe, the possibility of meeting the soul mate on earth would be extremely rare.

Major Arcanum XXI, representing successful transmutation and denoting the completion of the Great Work is aptly called THE ADEPT. The enlightening spiritual lesson revealed by this tarot card is limited only by the capacity of understanding of the viewer. Meditation on its splendid symbolism attunes one to the Source, revealing the reason for being, destiny, and how to handle individual potentials to gain from life the ultimate in happiness, usefulness, and spirituality.

The three letters at the bottom of the illustration are (1-r) Schine (Hebrew), S (English), and Sichen (Egyptian). At the top we find the corresponding number to be 21. The Roman numeral XXI designates the number of the Major Arcanum of the Egyptian tarot. The Sun is the astrological correspondence of the card. In divination, Arcanum XXI represents Success and Attainment.

A young girl, symbolizing purity of life, kneels while she plays the harp of three strings. Her kneeling position indicates absolute devotion to higher laws, and prayerful aspirations to live the life of the spirit. Her moderate garments, without decoration, portray simplicity of living and moderation in desires. The three strings on the harp signify harmony of the body, intellect, and emotions.

Composed of 12 flowers, the wreath above refers to the 12 signs of the zodiac in which all experience is gained. The three blossoms on each flower point out that both souls, their joining portrayed in the winged lingha in the center, have plucked the flowers of zodiacal experiences on all planes: Physical, astral, and spiritual.

Typifying the processes of evolution are the emblems around the zodiac of flowers. At each quadrant is a head; those of an eagle and a bull below, and a lion and a man above, taken from the fixed signs of the zodiac. These are Scorpio, Taurus, Leo, and Aquarius.

These emblems are the four forms of the Egyptian sphinx, also symbolizing the passage of the Sun through the four quadrants of the zodiac, or four seasons of the year. The ancient magi pointed the way to adeptship for the neophyte with this ensemble of pictographs. He must have energy and courage to sustain his efforts, knowledge to direct his energies properly, labor ceaselessly for the realization of his aspirations and tune his emotions to a higher, more spiritual vibratory level. In other words, he must develop four attributes; wisdom, perseverance, courage, and love.

Embracing these ideas is the familiar occult admonition: "To know, to do, to dare, to be silent."

These four heads were used to portray evolution. The head of the lion was picked because of its association with the creative forces of its solar sign, Leo, indicating the necessary courage for attaining real and lasting success.

The head of the bull associated with Taurus and representing the fructifying principle of nature, was chosen to emphasize that all progress is the result of labor.

The head of the eagle, associated with the higher expression of the zodiacal sign Scorpio, was used to indicate spirituality. The head of the man with a sacred serpent at his brow, indicating fertility and associated with Aquarius, was selected to symbolize both intuition and intelligence as necessary guides in the process of unfolding the highest spiritual possibilities.

In the center of the wreath composed of zodiacal flowers is a phallus (positive urges) and a yoni (negative forces) conjoined, sustained by two wings and soaring upward. This winged lingha symbolizes the permanent union of soul mates who ascend together into angelic realms.

Painting a symbolical picture of unlimited destiny, the ensemble is described by Zain:[3] "The girl kneeling by the harp denotes this union is brought about by living the life of the spirit while on earth." Spiritual aspirations and devotion to furthering God's Great Plan, loving and unselfish endeavor to contribute the utmost to cosmic welfare, together with a clear conception of the laws of harmony, in time bring about the recognition across spaces and the development of exchanging lines of force, which lead to this ineffable union. This harmonious reverberation of soul to soul is symbolized by the harp of three strings, for the union embraces all three planes.

"Strength depends upon harmony, and the music of their souls sounding across the spaces endows both with a hitherto unknown power to overcome obstacles, to gain the blossoms of experience on all three planes, as signified by the three flowers related to each of the 12 signs of the zodiac. As a whole the ensemble signifies the attainment of adeptship while on earth, and the crown of angelhood that awaits such perfect human beings when they have passed from the physical and function in the sublime vistas of the future."

Chapter XXII

The Neophyte's Spiritual Initiation

After years of investigating occult science, I am still amazed at the wealth of information to be gleaned from a study of the tarot where everything in the universe seems to be included. When some new factor comes to light, into the margin of attention, consulting the tarot brings deeper understanding. The discovery of another member in our planetary chain provides a splendid example.

The discovery of Pluto was announced January 21, 1930. Naturally this new astrological orb commanded the attention of astrologers and taroists. Many questions were stimulated in their minds.

What sign of the zodiac did Pluto rule? In what sign was it exalted, in its harmony or inharmony, or in its fall? What was its nature in terms of human behavior? How did it coincide with the thoughts, feelings and actions? Answers poured forth in numerous uncritical words, which meant nothing. But all agreed, after the study of events in general that Pluto's bow into objective consciousness was associated with extremes and groups.

If the ancients were right about the influence of this tenth planet in our realm, it exerts a mediumistic force similar to that of the Moon, only a more refined nature. Moving out from the Sun, Mercury is the first planet, and Uranus (the first discovered modern planet) is the octave influence of it. The next planet out from the Sun is Venus. Neptune, second discovered modern planet, is an octave expression of Venus.

Should this system be right, the third discovered new planet, Pluto, should have an influence which is the octave expression of the earth, whose influence is reflected by the Moon. The Moon, lower octave, represents the domestic urges in the subconscious mind (home, family, etc.) while Pluto, higher octave, extends to the universal welfare urges (a cosmic realization of everything in the universe as one family).

After some years of research astrologers are now more or less agreed on the rulership of Pluto. As far as I have been able to learn, the most active astrological researchers in the world can be found in America, England, France, Australia, and India. These groups allot the rulership of Pluto to the sign of Scorpio. Many consider Scorpio as a double-rulership sign in that they also allot Mars as a ruler of the sign. A few hold that Pluto rules Aries.

Sometimes this difference of opinion bothers students. The same situation occurs in all fields of knowledge. The only relief for such a confused attitude is for the student to learn to erect his precise horoscope and read it. Then he can, through his own research, make up his mind about the matter of rulership.

Fortunately there are many fine classes being conducted. Anyone living in this Aquarian Age certainly owes it to himself to take advantage of astrological study, a priceless spiritual freedom for which we can be thankful.

In the tarot, Pluto is associated with Arcanum XXII called THE MATERIALIST. The three letters at the bottom of the illustration are (1-r) Tau (Hebrew), T (English) and Toth (Egyptian). At the top we find the corresponding number to be 22. The Roman numeral XXII designates the number of the Major Arcanum of the Egyptian tarot. The astrological correspondence of the card is the planet Pluto.

Each tarot card relates to a distinct potential of the human soul and to one of the essential steps a neophyte must take to reach a climax of human possibilities. Arcanum XXII, like Pluto, has a dual interpretation.

A blind man is seen carrying bags on his left shoulder. These bags represent material things he has directed all of life's energies to acquiring, or they signify ability to use his divine potentials in physical assistance to the needy. Leaning on the black staff indicates experience with good and evil as he walks forward.

If he has attempted to live the life of the spirit, this symbolism portrays that his desire to help and protect others is so strong, he ignores danger in performing his good deeds. On the other hand, in the lower life expression it signifies that the fleshy, selfish appetites are so strong that self discipline (the way to the spirit) is lacking.

He approaches a fallen obelisk, which symbolizes the final overthrow of all temporal work and power. The open-mouthed crocodile, waiting to devour the man, pictures the ultimate fate of anyone who is blind to the spiritual things of life, a slave to his own desires.

Taken as a whole, the ensemble represents the inevitable suffering that follows sin. Or, if the higher side expresses, it symbolizes that the spiritual man enthusiastically doing all he can within his power to assist humanity, is completely blind to the consequences to himself.

Above the man is the eclipse in the sky, symbolizing that the inner spiritual light has been obscured by material interests when man functions on a low dominant vibratory rate. However, in the higher interpretation, the eclipse warns that the ever-ready inner plane dark forces (lower Pluto) may try shutting out the guiding current of the neophyte's spiritual illumination if he does not maintain a high dominant vibratory rate.

Thus through symbolical language did the ancient teachers in temples of learning explain to their pupils the law of compensation, which decrees that effort expended in constructive channels is always followed by increased ability and real advancement, both spiritual and material.

Since the discovery of Pluto, material science has concerned itself more and more with the inside workings of things to gain information about energies recognized for centuries by occultists. The result is that today occult law can be interpreted more readily in physical terms.

Take astrology, for instance. Each birth chart and progressed aspect between planets maps stimulated subconscious urges. The individual responds to the stimulation in a pleasurable or painful manner according to the nature of the aspect and his conditioning subsequent to birth. Response affects the glands of internal secretion harmoniously or discordantly due to this conditioning energy. Thus can we more easily explain astrology and health. It is not the planet that brings the event but the person's response to the corresponding stimulation in his mind, which is mapped by the planets.

Then, too, as each cell in the body is a battery developing wave lengths enabling it to contact the thought-cells of the inner plane, it is more easily understood how the soul moves progressively to a higher life form. This same knowledge of the interpenetration of energies from both planes reveals the true use of pleasure and pain in our lives. Nature uses these factors to educate and encourage us on the road to spiritual attainment.

Pluto, in astrology, has two distinct and opposite qualities. It signifies gangsters and racketeers on the adverse side and the highest type of spiritual effort on its better side; material selfishness or cosmic unselfishness.

Every life form on earth desires happiness. Perhaps there are as many definitions for happiness as there are life forms, because each, the sum total of its own individual experiences, desires something different. Yet, there seems to be a broad general approach to happiness which can be successfully practiced by anyone. The ancient teachers told in pictographs of important elements to be considered, and modern psychologists gave us the words to reinterpret what the ancient magi tried to convey.

Happiness can only be obtained by going out from oneself. This is a difficult task, because the out-going-ness must be some outside interest, because self centered minds are never happy. Usually too much thinking about self and the effect of everything upon oneself prevents the expression of the insistent urges within us. Only those who learn to go out from themselves are happy.

Anyone who has found the line of endeavor in which he can render greatest service to humanity, who has learned how to find pleasure in all that he does, who makes an effort to refine his body, intellect and feelings, and who has taken the time and pains to uncover harmonious channels (shown by a timed horoscope) for all his insistent desires, is one of the happiest people in the world.

That person has captured and utilized the higher expressed energies of the universal welfare urge mapped by the most recently discovered member of our planetary chain, Pluto. At this point his spiritual pathway toward adeptship takes him closer to being endowed with a neophyte's illumination.

Chapter XXIII

ASTROLOGY AND THE MINOR ARCANA

Plates of the ancients, handed down to the modern world as tarot cards, symbolized the knowledge of the secret schools embracing spiritual science and universal law. Of the 78 tarot cards, 22 contain the most important lessons for a neophyte. Preceding chapters have presented the spiritual message depicted by the 22 Major Arcana.

If you will permit me to use my Neptune thought-cells, I would like to share one of my day dreams with you. (Time will tell if this utopian stirring is a daydream or not.) Zain's *Ritual of Egyptian Initiation* is a vivid lesson for the occultist. My "dream" is to see this dramatic and inspiring initiation enacted in color on a wide screen, and as it unfolds to hear a commentary, a voice describing the content as appropriate pictures and symbols bleed one into another on that screen.

In that reference there is an account of the trials of initiation and of information give to the neophyte while passing the tests in the mysteries of ancient Egypt. Different steps in this initiation and what each step signifies is explained. During the initiation, the candidate is stopped before 22 frescoed paintings picturing the 22 Major Arcana of the tarot. He has to memorize the symbolism. The plates correspond to the 12 signs of the zodiac and the 10 planets. We moderns can apply the key of astrology to tarot philosophy and find a splendid guide for effectively meeting the trials of initiation as the soul in its pilgrimage spirals the pathway of evolution.

Recording still more knowledge about the numerical interaction of forces and ideas, the ancients added a scale of ten numerals: one, two, three, four, five, six, seven, eight, nine, 10. The numerals were repeated in association with the emblems of the four kingdoms (fire, earth, air, and water), making a total of 40 more plates, called the Minor Arcana. The four elements correspond to the four suits of 10 cards each.

An ancient, rare work inscribed on palm leaves, the *Atma Bodha*, presents in *Book III, The Aphoresmata of the Logos*, this statement: "Whatever exists, exists as a Whole, as God, or as a part, or emanation from God." One represents the Whole, the Beginning, the End, a universal truth represented by Major Arcanum I. A bible quotation from Rev. 22:12: "I am the Alpha and Omega, the beginning and the end, the first and the last" explains Major Arcanum I which, not surprisingly, pictures symbols of the four Minor Arcana suits: Scepters, Cups, Swords, and Coins.

Environmental factors resisting the notions of early peoples left their imprint on and were involved in the origin of the suits. The most important natural phenomena, the passing of the seasons, provided the emblems.

Coins

In spring, life bursts forth, bringing a new food supply to nourish the waiting world. However, food necessary to sustain life had to be purchased, so pieces of money were developed (coins). From this exchange of money for food stems the origin of the suit of coins. Representing

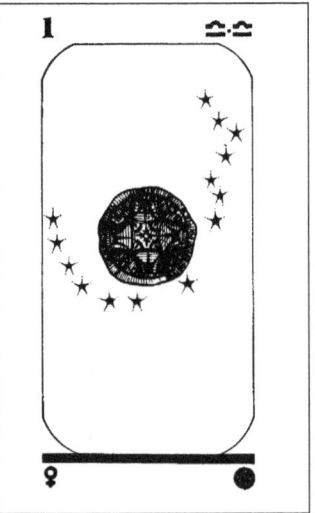

balmy spring air, the coins correspond to the airy signs of the zodiac, and air is the most essential food of life.

But money was needed for other purchases in those days. So when commercialism permeated later times, more and more trade replaced the actual coin. As diamonds were considered more precious than money, this social trend replaced the coin with the diamond on modern playing cards. Money has become the symbol of life itself, Astrologically, the coins correspond to the Ascendant in the birth chart, the place where each newborn day rises at the eastern horizon.

Scepters

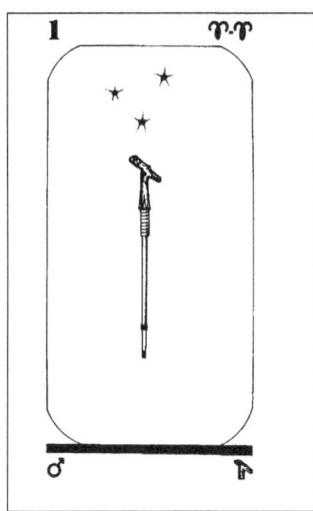

In summer, heat brought the three-leaf clover, important food for the flocks of early pastorial people. Because of the importance of a continued food supply, it was natural for them to link the clover to this season. From this concept stems the origin of the emblem used for the suit of scepters. The fiery heat of summer came to be represented by scepters, which correspond to the fiery signs of the zodiac.

Experience taught other peoples a similar heat could be produced by wood. Therefore, the picture of clover on modern playing cards is referred to as clubs. In human life the element of fire expresses as enthusiasm, ambition, and enterprise. Consequently, it is associated with business, occupation, station, honor, and profession. In astrology, scepters correspond to the birth chart Midheaven, the place of the Sun at noon.

Cups

Autumn, when grapes were pressed for wine, provided the season for festivities, dancing, marriage. These activities deeply stirred the emotions of the early population, so they danced barefooted in the huge tubs of grapes, performing one of the earliest pressing operations. Here again the transition from ancient to modern emphasis is clearly indicated. Early people used the emblem of a wine cup to symbolize the vivid emotions aroused by the activities in autumn. The sociological trend provided the origin of the emblem used for the suit of cups. Cups correspond to the watery signs of the zodiac.

However, moderns, not living so close to the land, associated joyous emotions of the heart with the rite of marriage, and used the heart as the symbol on playing cards. The water element symbolizes emotion. It is typical of domestic and affectional relations. Thus, in a broad astrological sense, the cups correspond to the birth chart Descendant, the place where the sun sinks below the western horizon.

Swords

In winter, a time of death and want, early peoples were hard put to gather and hoard sufficient food to last until spring. Observation revealed to them that the oak tree grew acorns which the squirrel hoarded against the barren winter. But as time passed, it proved increasingly difficult for people to meet the demands of the season. Irritation developed, tempers flared, and groups entered into conflict. Gradually the mental concept of the season changed to an idea of strife, symbolized by the sword. Social pressure instigated

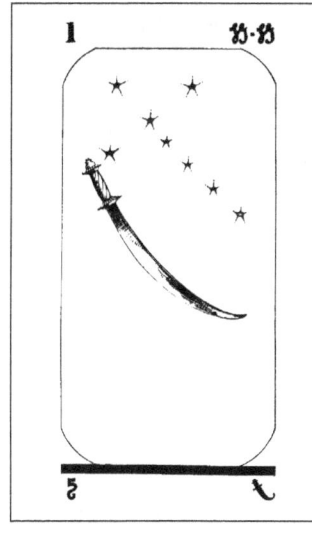 change offering the origin of the emblem used for the suit of swords.

Representing the hardships of winter, this suit corresponds to the earth signs of the zodiac. A still later people used the modern emblem of toil, a spade, to indicate the drudgery inflicted upon them during the unfruitful winter. Thus swords were replaced by spades on playing cards. Symbolizing struggles associated with affliction and death, swords correspond to the birth chart Nadir, the place where the sun is in its grave, lowest diurnal cycle point.

Decanates

In astrology, we divide each 30 degrees, a zodiacal sign, into three decanates of 10 degrees each. Taken as a whole, the sign represents a definite type of motivation. Then each of its decanates has a shading of its own corresponding to the zodiacal triplicity of the sign element.

For instance, Aries, one sign of the fiery triplicity, embraces three decanates sub-ruled by Aries, Leo, and Sagittarius. If a planet is located in the last 10 degrees of Aries, its falls in the third or Sagittarius decanate. This maps motivation which has a tendency to express in a Jupiterian manner (Jupiter rules Sagittarius). Although the strongest impress upon action is signified by Aries, the Jupiter decanate position maps a shading of motivation differing from that of, say, the Leo (second) decanate.

The 12 signs of the zodiac are divided into four triplicities: Fire (Aries, Leo, Sagittarius), earth (Taurus, Virgo, Capricorn), air (Gemini, Libra, Aquarius) and water (Cancer, Scorpio, Pisces).

Just as the decanates refer to the zodiacal signs, in the tarot there is a similar relationship between the Minor Arcana and the Major Arcana. The exoteric divinitory significance of the Minor Arcana is derived from the numerical relation to the Major Arcana. Each Minor Arcana portrays an esoteric, spiritual significance tied in with the corresponding decanate division of the zodiac. Thus, the key which unlocks the meaning of either Arcana, Major or Minor, is astrology. Let us consider each suit from the numerical relationship.

The Aces

From astrology we have learned that Mercury is associated with study, writing, correspondence and travel. As the Aces (1) correspond numerically to Mercury and Major Arcanum I, when read from common divination they relate to one of those things, according to the particular department of life as designated by the suit. However, in readings for spiritual development, they can be interpreted in terms of the first decanate of each zodiacal triplicity, starting with the signs of the movable (or cardinal) quality.

The 12 zodiacal signs are also divided into three qualities. The movable (Cardinal) quality embraces Aries, Cancer, Libra and Capricorn. The mutable (or common) quality consists of Gemini, Virgo, Sagittarius and Pisces. The fixed quality is expressed in Taurus, Leo, Scorpio and Aquarius.

To facilitate the reading of the minor aces in a tarot spread, here is the significance of each.

Ace of Scepters: News of a business opportunity. Inner Interpretation: Activity (first decanate of Aries).

Ace of Cups: Letter from a loved one. Inner interpretation: Moods (first decante of Cancer).

Ace of Coins: A short journey. Inner interpretation: Policy (first decante of Libra).

Ace of Swords: News of sickness or death. Inner interpretation: (first decante of Capricorn).

Chapter XXIV

DIVINITORY SIGNIFICANCE

Fred Skinner, one of the outstanding taroists of this century said: "Astrology puts the meat on the bones of the tarot." A vivid statement implying that if one is not combined with the other, both astrology and the tarot suffer.

If we consider the universe in all her manifestations as being under law, then this law must invariably be based upon mathematical principles. Mathematical relations are absolute, pertaining to spiritual, celestial and angelic realms as well as Earth. God geometrizes. Everything, from the ripple of a thought to the evolution of a universe, operates strictly according to numerical law. As above, so below.

Mathematics alone enables a person to avoid mental pitfalls. It is due to this fact that the golden key (astrology) and the silver key (tarot) are the most valuable possessions that the occult student can obtain in the world of mental research. They are grounded in and strictly built upon numerical proportions.

In previous chapters we have seen the strict correspondence between the 22 Major Arcanum and the 10 planets and the 12 signs of the zodiac. The Minor Arcana correspond to the 36 decanates and the four elements.

Each zodiacal sign is divided into three equal sections, called decanates. Therefore, in each quadrant of the zodiac there are nine decanates. These nine belong to one of the four elements, the triplicities of fire, earth, air, and water. The tenth or transitional factor represents the element to which the nine decanates belong, being distributed in the three signs making up one of the zodiacal triplicities.

In the last chapter we ended with the divinitory significance of the Aces of the Minor Arcana. Here is the interpretation of the other nine cards for each suit.

Deuces

From astrology we have learned that Virgo signifies science and labor. As the deuces (two) correspond numerically to Virgo and Major Arcanum II, when read for common divination they relate to those things according to the particular department of life indicated by the suit. However, in reading for spiritual development, they can be interpreted in terms of the second decanate of each zodiacal triplicity, starting with the movable (cardinal) signs.

Deuce of Scepters: Business depending upon scientific methods. Inner interpretation: Exaltation (second decanate Aries).

Deuce of Cups: A work of love. Inner interpretation: Revelation (second decanate Cancer).

Deuce of Coins: Money acquired by hard labor. Inner interpretation: Independence (second decanate Libra).

Deuce of Swords: Sickness through overwork. Inner interpretation: Martyrdom (second decanate Capricorn).

Treys

Libra signifies partnership, open enemies, lawsuits and dealing with the public. As the treys (three) correspond numerically to Libra and Major Arcanum III, when read for common divination they relate to these things according to the particular department of life indicated by the suit. However, in reading for spiritual development, they can be interpreted in terms of the third decanate of each zodiacal triplicity, starting with the movable signs.

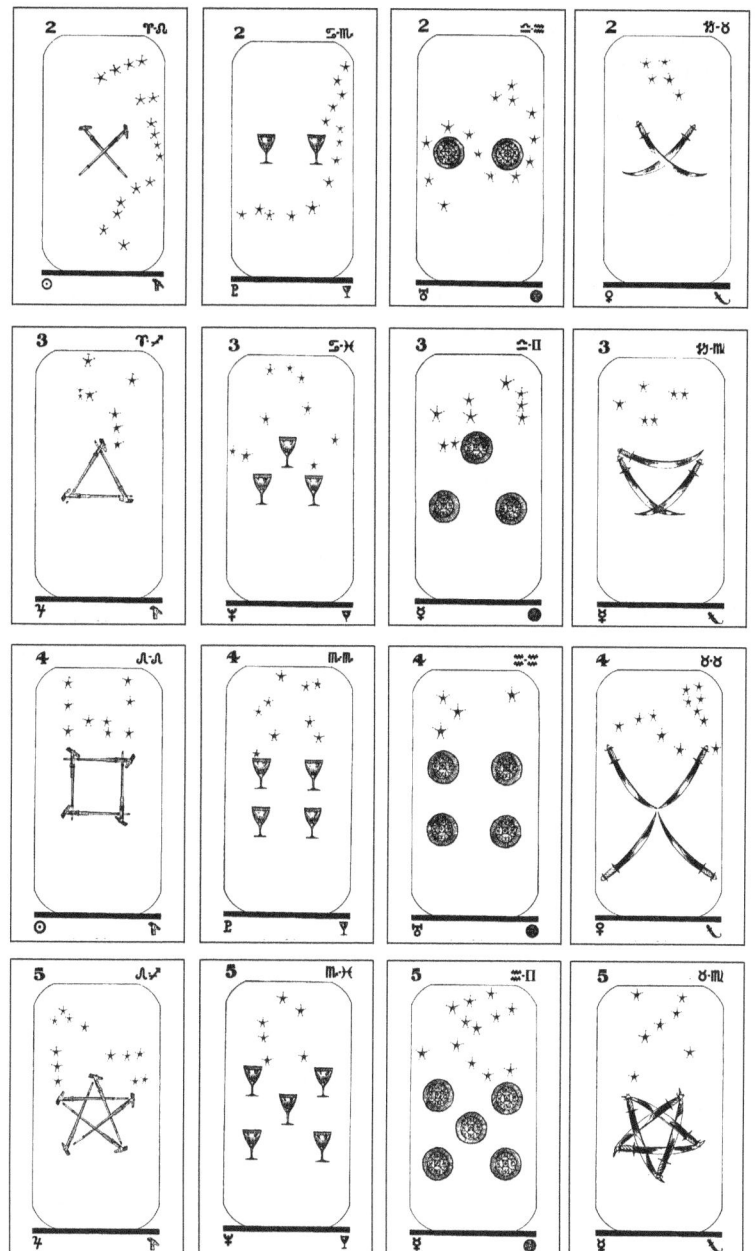

Trey of Scepters: A business partnership. Inner interpretation: Propaganda (third decanate Aries).

Trey of Cups: A marriage for love. Inner interpretation: Research (third decanate Cancer).

Trey of Coins: A marriage for money. Inner interpretation: Expiration (third decanate Libra).

Trey of Swords: A lawsuit or divorce. Inner interpretation: Idealism (third decanate Capricorn).

Fours

Scorpio signifies fruitfulness, legacies, spirit communion, the dead, and the partner's money. As the fours correspond numerically to Scorpio and Major Arcanum IV, they relate to these things according to the particular phase of life indicated by the suit. However, in reading for spiritual development, they can be interpreted in terms of the fourth decanate of each zodiacal triplicity, starting the count with the movable (cardinal) signs.

Four of scepters: A legacy. Inner interpretation: Rulership (first decanate Leo).

Four of Cups: An increase in the family. Inner interpretation: Resourcefulness (first decanate Scorpio).

Four of Coins: Money received through a partner. Inner interpretation: Originality (first decanate Aquarius).

Four of Swords: Remorse for past action. Inner interpretation: Determination (first decanate Taurus).

Fives

Astrologically, Jupiter signifies good fortune. As the fives correspond numerically to Jupiter and the Major Arcanum V, when read for common divination they relate to good luck in reference to the particular department of life indicated by the suit. However, their higher interpretation is revealed by the fifth decanate of each zodiacal triplicity, starting with the moveable (cardinal) signs.

Five of Scepters: Good fortune in business. Inner interpretation: Reformation (second decanate Leo).

Five of cups: Good fortune in love. Inner interpretation: Responsibility (second decanate Scorpio).

Five of Coins: Abundant wealth. Inner interpretation: Inspiration (second decanate Aquarius).

Five of Swords: Escape from danger. Inner interpretation: Struggle (second decanate Taurus).

Sixes

Venus rules love, art, music, drama, and the social functions. As the sixes correspond to Venus and Major Arcanum VI, they relate to these things in reference to the particular phase of life represented by the suit. However, their higher interpretation can be read in terms of the sixth decanate of each zodiacal triplicity, starting with the movable signs.

Six of Scepters: Music, art, or drama. Inner interpretation: Ambition (third decanate Leo).

Six of Cups: A love affair. Inner interpretation: Attainment (third decanate of Scorpio).

Six of Coins: A social event. Inner Interpretation: Repression (third decante Aquarius).

Six of Swords: Dissipation. Inner interpretation: Mastership (third decanate Taurus).

Sevens

Corresponding numerically to Major Arcanum VII and Sagittarius, significator of philosophy, long journeys, publishing, teaching, and outdoor sports, the sevens relate to them in conjunction with whatever phase of life is indicated by the suit. The inner

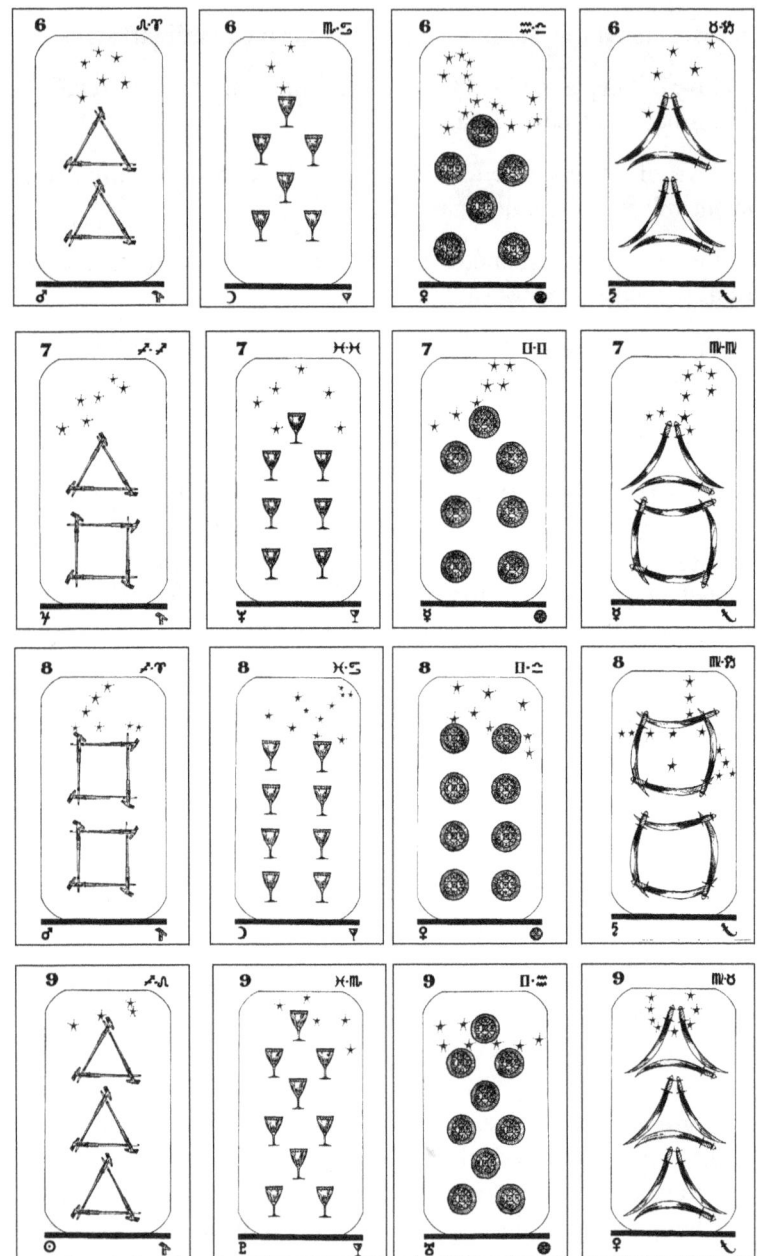

influence is revealed by the seventh decanate of each triplicity, starting the count with the movable signs.

Seven of Scepters: Success in teaching and in publishing. Inner interpretation: Devotion (first decanate Sagittarius).

Seven of Cups: A successful change of home. Inner interpretation: Verity (first decanate Pisces).

Seven of Coins: Money earned through a journey. Inner interpretation: Intuition (first decanate Gemini).

Seven of Swords: Danger through travel or sport. Inner interpretation: Achievement (first decanate Virgo).

Eights

Corresponding numerically to Arcanum VIII and Capricorn, significator of station, honor, business, and government affairs, the eights relate to these things in association with the phase of life designated by the suit. The inner interpretation is revealed by the eighth decanate of each triplicity starting with the movable signs.

Eight of Scepters: A political appointment. Inner interpretation: Exploration (second decanate Sagittarius).

Eight of Cups: Extravagance. Inner interpretation: Self-sacrifice (second decanate Pisces).

Eight of Coins: A costly lawsuit. Inner interpretation: Fidelity (second decanate Gemini).

Eight of Swords: Loss of honor. Inner interpretation: Experience (second decanate Virgo).

Nines

Astrologically, Aquarius signifies friends, associates, hopes, and wishes. Thus the nines, corresponding numerically to Aquarius and Major Arcanum IX, relate to these things in association with the department of life designated by the suit. Inner interpretation is revealed by the ninth decanate of each zodiacal triplicity, starting the count with the movable signs.

Nine of Scepters: Wise and profitable friendship. Inner interpretation: Illumination (third decanate Leo).

Nine of Cups: Hopes will be realized. Inner interpretation: Vicissitudes (third decanate Pisces). The nine of cups is called the wish card.

Nine of Coins: Money spent on associates. Inner interpretation: Reason (third decanate Gemini.)

Nine of Swords: Quarrel resulting in enmity. Inner interpretation: Renunciation: (third decanate Virgo).

Tens

In astrology Uranus signifies uncommon pursuits, sudden changes of fortune, inventions, discoveries, and unconventional relations and actions. The tens, corresponding numerically to Uranus and Major Arcanum X, relate to these things in the department of life indicated by the suit. Inner interpretation: Tens can be read according to the zodiacal triplicities in their elemental relationship.

Tens of Scepters: An invention or discovery. Inner interpretation: Enthusiasm (air).

Ten of Cups: Unconventional affectional interest. Inner inter-

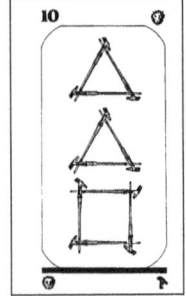  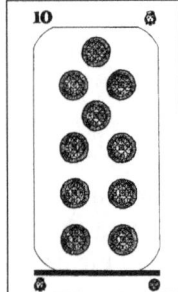 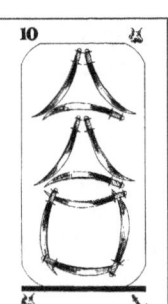

pretation: Emotion (water).

Ten of Coins: Alternate financial loss and gain. Inner interpretation: Aspiration (fire).

Ten of Swords: Sudden loss of employment. Inner interpretation: Practicality (earth).

A study of spiritual astrology will provide the depth of meaning to the keyword given for the higher significance of each Minor Arcana. On every tarot card there appears an astrological symbol. The more that is known about the meaning behind the symbol, the more the scope of interpretation is increased through the law of correspondences.

Chapter XXV

The Tarot Face Cards

As the tarot is a symbolical synthesis of the universe, all of its component parts can be understood by applying universal language to it. Astrological symbolism, comprising this universal language, is the key unlocking the meaning of each part. Therefore, each card must correspond to an astrological factor.

In previous chapters we have seen the strict correspondence between the 22 Major Arcanum and the 10 planets and the 12 signs of the zodiac, and between the Minor Arcana and the 36 decanates of the zodiacal signs, and the 4 elements their triplicities represents.

Spiritual science and universal law express the numerical interaction of forces and ideas between the four kingdoms of fire, earth, air and water, depicted in the major and Minor Arcana. All forces in the universe have an influence upon man, their focal point. However, human beings are not all the same. The different types are clearly expressed by the sign of the zodiac under which each person is born.

Using universal symbolism, the ancient magi fashioned another 12 plates, or tarot cards, picturing people born under each of the zodiacal signs. To convey the family unit and relationship, they drew a father, mother and son, more commonly called the king, queen, and youth (jack). They associated a tarot suit with these people to show their temperaments.

Aside from the cosmic and other radiations by which man is

surrounded, there is another imponderable force of great importance. His own thoughts and the thoughts of others had to be represented in the series of plates. To show that these thoughts originated with people, the ancients pictured four tarot cards as horsemen.

In those early days the Twins, in astrology associated with the third house of private thoughts by the horoscope, were often portrayed riding horses. In addition, Sagittarius, natural ruler of the ninth house of publicly expressed thoughts, is a horseman.

There are 14 Court Arcana. The 12 common Court Arcana describe people born under each of the 12 signs of the zodiac. The four court cards signify the type of influence each person exerts through his thoughts.

Therefore, the complete set of tarot plates consists of 22 Major Arcana, 40 Minor Arcana, and 16 Court Arcana: A total of 78 cards.

Because they represent all of humanity, both men and women, born under the 12 zodiacal signs, the king, queen, and youth of each suit have a numerical value of 10 each. Man alone or woman alone is represented by the number five.

But each Court Arcana not only signifies a person of the sex pictured on the card of a given temperament, it also signifies, when reversed, one of the opposite sex of that temperament, thus giving two fives, or 10 for the whole card. Strictly speaking, either the king, queen, or youth is numerically 10.

The Kings

The kings represent action, or the first degree of emanation of each zodiacal triplicity.

King of scepters signifies a person ruled by the sign Aries: Fiery, headstrong, ambitious, courageous, and energetic. Right way up in a tarot spread, it means an Aries man; reversed, an Aries woman. The dominant motivating principle behind the person's

actions is I AM.

King of Swords signifies a person ruled by the sign Taurus: Reserved, sullen, and practical. Right way up, a Taurus man; reversed, a Taurus woman. The Dominant motivation is I HAVE.

King of Coins signifies a person ruled by the sign Gemini: Intelligent, restless, changeable, and fickle. Right way up, a Gemini man; reversed, a Gemini woman. Dominant idea is I THINK.

King of Cups signifies a person ruled by the sign of Cancer: Mild, reserved, home-loving, and pleasant. Right way up it means a Cancer man; reversed, a Cancer woman. Motivating key is I FEEL.

In addition to temperament, the astrological symbols on the cards point to a general personal description. *Aries:* Middle stature, spare, strong body, busy eyebrows, dark hair, rather swarthy. *Taurus:* Short, thickset, dull complexion, large mouth, dark hair and eyes. *Gemini:* Tall, long arms, light complexion, brown hair, quick in action. *Cancer:* Middle height, upper parts of body larger, small mouth and face, milky eyes.

In spreading a spread of tarot cards, a king turning up gives clues to the type of person (as well as the general physical description) who has something to do with the answer to whatever question was asked before the cards were spread. So it is with the other face cards of the tarot.

The Queens

The queens represent reaction, or the second degree of emanation of each triplicity.

Queen of Scepters denotes a person ruled by the zodiacal sign of Leo: Haughty, high spirited, ambitious, and resolute. Right way up it signifies a Leo woman; reversed, a Leo man. Strong motivation behind action is I WILL.

Queen of Swords signifies a person ruled by the sign Virgo: Studious, rather even tempered, ingenious, and witty. Right way up it means a Virgo woman; reversed, a Virgo man. Dominant motivation is I ANALYZE.

Queen of coins shows a person ruled by the sign Libra: Good, high-minded, noble and compliant. Right way up it indicates a Libra woman; reversed, a Libra man. I BALANCE is the dominant motivation.

Queen of Cups signifies a person ruled by the sign Scorpio: Active, selfish, proud, resentful, reserved, and thoughtful. Right way up it shows a Scorpio woman; reversed, a Scorpio man. The dominant idea is I DESIRE.

Personal description of each of these types will assist in recognizing the particular person indicated by the queens. *Leo:* Breadth and size to stature, large head, light hair, ruddy complexion. *Virgo:* Average, compact body, brownish or fresh complexion, dark hair. *Libra:* Tall and well-formed, clear complexion, sparkling eyes, hair brown or black. *Scorpio:* Middle height, thickset, corpulent, hooked nose, dark hair, ruddy or swarthy complexion.

The Youths

The youths, products of action and reaction, represent the third degree of emanation of each triplicity. The horsemen do not represent people. As thoughts are ruled by Arcanum I, each horseman has a numerical value of one.

Youth of Scepters denotes a person ruled by the sign Sagittarius: Benevolent, free, jovial, quick tempered, energetic, and fond of outdoor sports. Right way up it denotes a Sagittarius man; reversed, a Sagittarius woman. Dominant idea is I SEE.

Youth of Swords signifies a person ruled by the sign Capricorn: Crafty, subtle, reserved, and greedy. Right way up it denotes a Capricorn man; reversed, a Capricorn woman. Motivation stems from the I USE motive.

Youth of Coins denotes a person ruled by the sign of Aquarius: Witty, argumentative yet friendly, artistic, humanitarian, and fond of refined company. Right way up it denotes an Aquarian man; reversed, an Aquarian woman. Dominant motivation is I KNOW.

Youth of Cups shows a person ruled by the sign of Pisces: Negative, timid, listless, harmless, and greatly influenced by the company he keeps. Right way up it denotes a Pisces man; reversed, a

Pisces woman. Strong idea behind thought and action is I BELIEVE.

The zodiacal sign in the upper right corner of each of the cards gives a clue to the person's physical description. *Sagittarius:* Above middle height, high forehead, long nose, sanguine complexion, brown hair. *Capricorn:* Slender rather than stout, thin face, black hair, dark complexion. *Aquarius*: Stout, fair hair, sanguine complexion, pleasant and solid looking. *Pisces:* Tending to shortness, fleshy, pale face, brown or dark hair, dreamy eyes.

The Horsemen

Horsemen of the Egyptian tarot represent people as do the other Court Arcana, but they signify thoughts of unseen intelligences. In a tarot spread, they are interpreted as thoughts having an impact upon the life of the person receiving the reading. The person who thinks the thoughts is shown by the Major Arcanum that turns up in the spread nearest the horseman.

Horseman of Scepters indicates thoughts concerning business. If the card falls right way up, beneficial thoughts are denoted. Reversed, thoughts opposed to business interests.

Horseman of Swords shows thoughts of enmity, strife, or sickness. Right way up it indicates thoughts devoted to the defense and protection of the person. Reversed, plans and desires for his ruin.

Horseman of Coins relates to thoughts of health or money.

Right way up, these thoughts have a tendency to attract money. Reversed, they involve plots to get money by foul means.

Horseman of Cups signifies thoughts of love and affection. Right way up, they are sincere and to the advantage of the person for which the reading is given. Reversed, they denote deceit or opposition to the true affectional desires.

To determine the influence upon the life of any of the Court Arcana, it is necessary to consider the card just preceding it in the spread. To learn what action will be taken in regards to the question asked, or to determine any moves made by the person represented by a Court Arcana, the card following it in the spread should be consulted.

When the tarot cards are spread to answer spiritual and philosophical problems the Court Arcana represent 12 zodiacal signs and the things they rule, much as the 12 types of intelligences. The horsemen indicate the four elemental kingdoms. They should be read as possible influences to modify conditions.

Because a spread can be read from three planes (physical, astral, and spiritual) it is necessary to determine to what level the question belongs. Then keep the premises and conclusions on the same plane.

If the question is asked properly, the elements of its answer are within it. The tarot can be used to answer all kinds of questions when one acquires the proficiency that comes from much practice and checking the results. Examples of spreads can be found in the book *How to Read Tarot Cards*.[6]

Because everything that exists has an astrological counterpart with a tarot card, by selecting the proper factors, any physical, or occult problem may be solved by the use of the tarot in addition to astrology, the two keys that unlock the secrets of nature.

www.ingramcontent.com/pod-product-compliance
Lightning Source LLC
Chambersburg PA
CBHW020803160426
43192CB00006B/422